Running Barefoot

Women Write the Land

Wynne Edwards
Dianne Linden
Editors

Cover photo: Darrel Kajati
Cover design: John Luckhurst
Interior Design: Lorrie Chaher
Printed and bound in Canada by Priority Printing Ltd.

Rowan Books gratefully acknowledges the support of the Canada Council and the
Alberta Foundation for the Arts for our publishing program.

The following pieces in this collection have been previously published:

"Click Beetle," Valerie Stetson, *Gaspereau Review*, (No. 11, Spring 2000).

"Cutstalks in her Arms," Mary Maxwell, in *Descant*, (Vol. 32, No. 1, Spring, 2001).

"Divining," "Learning to Read," Shirley Serviss, in *Reading Between the Lines*,
Rowan Books, 2000.

"foreclosure," Doris Bircham, in *Riding the Northern Range*, Red Deer College Press,
1993, and *Cowgirls: 100 Years of Writing the Range*, Red Deer College Press, 1997.

"Fossils Waiting," Cathy Hodgson, in *Making Waves: An Ecumenical Feminist Journal*,
(Vol. 1, No. 4, Summer 2001).

"Learning the Land," Eunice Victoria Scarfe, in *Other Voices*, (June, 1998).

"Life as Prayer," Melody McKellar, in *Making Waves: An Ecumenical Feminist Journal*,
(Vol. 1, No. 4, Summer 2001).

"Making Our Way by Heart," Ruth Blaser, in *Making Waves: An Ecumenical Feminist
Journal*, (Vol. 1, No. 4, Summer 2001).

"My Utopia," p. k. Chamberlain, in *English*, (Vol. 33, No. 2, Fall 1995) and *Western People*,
(No. 926, January 29, 1998).

"Qu'Appelle Valley", Jacqueline Bell, in *Vintage 96*, League of Canadian Poets, Quarry Press.

"Sand Hills and Sage," Elsie Ellis, in *Sand Hills and Sage*, Prairie Lily Co-op, Saskatoon,
1998 and Harvest, Fifth House, Saskatoon, 1992, and The Land of My Undoing,
Sand Print, Hazlet, 1998.

"This Land Eats Things," Kerry Mulholland, in *Making Waves: An Ecumenical Feminist
Journal*, (Vol. 1, No. 4, Summer 2001).

"Upstream," "Buckhorn Mountains," Linda Wikene Johnson, in *Showcase Animals*,
Press Porcepic.

"What I have left is imagining," Heather MacLeod, in *Prairie Fire* (Vol. 12, No. 3) and
Shapes of Orion, Smoking Lung Press, 2000.

National Library of Canada Cataloguing in Publication Data

Main entry under title:

Running barefoot

ISBN 0-9685257-9-2

1. Canadian literature (English)--21st century.* 2. Canadian literature (English)--Women
authors.* I. Edwards, Wynne Margaret, 1943- II. Linden, Dianne.
PS8235.W7R86 2001   C810.8'09287   C2001-911100-2
PR9194.5.W6R86 2001

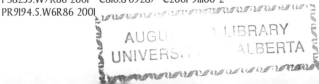

Dedication

*To Carolyn McDade,
whose voice and vision
have inspired this collection.*

Table of Contents

Section III - Breaking the Web   47

Section IV - Seeing in the Dark   73

Section V - From Generation to Generation   104

Acknowledgements

We are thankful to Carolyn McDade for her consistent emotional and practical support of this anthology and for the generous use of her music. We would also like to thank Audrey Brooks, Nancy Steeves, Carol Vogler and the other members of the anthology committee for their support and enthusiasm for this project.

Without the ongoing commitment of Rowan Books and in particular Heather Marshall through the past two years this anthology would not be in print. Christine Downing provided copyediting assistance.

We thank Marian Shatto for providing the beautiful handwritten notation for the songs used in this book. We are also grateful to the women who, with the guidance of Martha Cole, assembled the quilt, part of which is pictured on the cover. Darrel Kajati took the original photograph.

Finally we would like to thank the ever-growing sacred web of women who write, sing, speak, photograph, paint, or quilt their love of this land, and especially those whose contributions appear in the pages of this book.

ॐ

Foreword

Wynne Edwards

For many years Carolyn McDade has journeyed from the salt marshes of Cape Cod to the western parts of Canada to share her music and with it her visions of social justice. In the unfolding of these journeys, she has grown to love the Western Canadian landscape and the women who live within it. One winter evening she shared with the organizers of her Canadian gatherings her dream of recording the voices of the women who lived on the land she had grown to love.

They responded with enthusiasm, and after much initial planning, a network of women within the four western provinces began to gather in small and then larger groups to learn music Carolyn created for them. During the year that these women continued to learn Carolyn's music, some of the women began to express their experience of Carolyn's music through other art forms. Photographs, paintings and soft sculptures appeared at rehearsals. A collaborative quilt began to take shape when fabric artists from each of the western provinces prepared a seed square depicting each province.

From the same transformative energy that produced wonderful paintings, photographs and quilt blocks, the idea of a body of writing to accompany the recording project emerged. I was invited to share my writing and editing experience with the ever-increasing tribe who called themselves *women of the sacred web.*

I began attending rehearsals with the women from the Edmonton area. Sitting at the back of the room, I tried to translate into prose or poetry the experience of listening to the voices of women whose beautiful sound enthralled me, tried to discern what place there was for a written record in this powerful experience of music and text. In the summer of 1999, still unsure of my role, I joined eighty-eight women who travelled from the four western Canadian provinces as well as from Massachusetts and Pennsylvania in the United States, who gathered at the Banff Centre for the Performing Arts. There began the preparation that would end in the recording of the music for the compact disc *We Are the Land We Sing.*

Near the rehearsal room and recording studio, several smaller rooms were allocated to other purposes. A hand-painted sign identified one of these rooms as *The Writing Room.* It was here that a space was created where other writers on breaks from their singing responsibilities could join me to participate in small group writing exercises, exchange ideas about writing, or simply sit and write uninterrupted. Next door to the writing space, in the fabric arts area, many creative minds and hands assembled the collaborative quilt.

Initially in the writing room there was a flurry of creative activity. Then as the week progressed and rehearsals gave way to recording, work on the music became more intense. If we were not singing or working on the quilt we were asked to help those singing: to offer encouragement, and provide an ambience to offset the necessary technical accoutrements. At the end of the week the recording was finished, the quilt shone completed on the wall of the rehearsal room, but the writing project was on hold.

I departed from Banff with many fragments of writing done during that week, a few stories contributed from earlier writing, and many promises of writing to come. I wondered where the project would go, in what form it would survive, if indeed it would survive. I was pulled in the direction of an anthology of women's writings but how would it emerge from such a small beginning?

I didn't need to worry. Like its sister the quilt, the book soon acquired a life of its own. Since Banff the quilt has crisscrossed the continent, providing a centrepiece for connection for women gathered in Nova Scotia, on Cape Cod, at Harvard Divinity School, in the Qu'Appelle Valley, on the California coast, and at the six launches of *We Are the Land We Sing* held across the western provinces.

By October of 1999 when we launched the CD in Edmonton, the concept of a written record to accompany it had evolved into a plan to publish a collection of writing about women's spiritual connection to the land. Heather Marshall and Debbie Culbertson of Rowan Books were in the audience at the launch where I shared this latest vision. At the end of the evening they came forward and offered to publish our anthology.

Although there were willing writers among the women of the sacred web, it became clear that a volume of quality writing would require many more submissions than that group could provide. Those of us involved in discussion at that time also wanted to engender new ideas with the collection, to reach and involve more women. Five Edmonton women who had been at the Banff recording and were enthusiastic about the writing project formed an anthology committee. Dianne and I accepted editorial responsibility for what we now called *The Anthology*. Women from the other western provinces agreed to act as contact persons for their province.

Immediately after the call for submissions went out, work began to trickle in. Closer to deadline the trickle became a flood. Then began the bittersweet task of deciding which pieces somehow formed a unified whole, which pieces had to be rejected. Dianne and I spent countless hours searching for emergent themes in the writing and deciding which pieces fit within these themes. Eventually six sections emerged, each headed by a fragment of one of Carolyn McDade's songs which best represented that theme. It seemed natural to follow that page with lyrics for the entire song and then the notation by Marian Shatto. After those initial decisions were made, our work as editors was to assure ourselves and our publisher that the writing was the best it could be, while assuring the authors that it still said what they wanted it to say. A challenge we faced daily was editing those pieces that came from early members of the sacred web so they affirmed the work of these women without excluding readers who had not shared their experiences. I hope we have achieved this balance.

Whatever its origins, this book is ultimately written for everyone who loves the earth, who mourns its dwindling rain forests, the decline of its natural habitats, the places where water is made dangerous for drinking or washing. It is my hope that readers although recognizing vast problems that need to be reconciled, will also be inspired or affirmed. I hope also that as they are engaged in story, they will recognize and enjoy the examples of fine writing contained in this anthology.

ᔐ

ॐ

I
Earth Prayers

We are the land we sing
We are the prayer we bring
To these wide miles of morning.

Morning
Carolyn McDade

Morning

© 1998 by Carolyn McDade

As east-ern wa-ters turn their is-lands to the sun
the grass-es lift and fill a mess-age to the hills

the shore-land for-est em-bers a flow thrugh wood-ed shield
the wood-lands rise to moun-tains a-cross the ice and ledge

to pour a gold-en yield the prai-rie wide with morn-ing
as Earth re-news a pledge to lean these slopes toward morn-ing

Running Barefoot

Morning

Carolyn McDade

As eastern waters turn
their islands to the sun
the shoreland forest embers

A flow through wooded shield
to pour a golden yield
the prairie wide with morning

The grasses lift and fill
a message to the hills -
the woodlands rise to mountains

Across the ice and ledge
as Earth renews a pledge
to lean these slopes toward morning

Through slow descending green
a fragile wild, serene
to sheen the western waters

To shine through mist and rain
on island seas again -
the shore of tall trees standing

A continent in song
a planet spinning on
through waking miles of morning

The darkness follows soon
the reach and yield of moon
as stars reveal our passage

The old night reaching deep
to hold within its sleep
a land of dream and promise

This life, a blessing come
by turning to and from
the star that gives us morning

Were we to love as far
as shines this humble star
that kindles green in passing

Spirit of Earth and Wind
Spirit of Life within
may we be true in passing

We are the land we sing
we are the prayer we bring
to these wide miles of morning

A continent in song,
a planet singing on
the wide, wide miles of morning

We are the land we sing
we are the prayer we bring
to these wide miles of morning

A continent in song
a planet singing on
the wide wide miles of morning

Prairie Crocuses

Theresa Shea

At first a shock, like the lone
coyote rooted at the coulee's
lip, leaving tufts
of winter when he twirls
and flees.

Then the eye attunes, targets
the modest addition
to taupe, freezes
on the sudden purple intrusions
so tiny, so frail
that shock still.

From the Coulee at Dusk, Deliberately Approaching

Theresa Shea

Nobody records the calligraphy
etched by the porcupine's green-
black quills
as he lumbers to de-bark
the plumpest tree
fastidiously
and without haste.

Life as Prayer

Melody McKellar

From the moment I open my eyes in the morning, until I close them to sleep at night, I try to live my life as a prayer. Every thought, every action, every breath that I take connects with all of creation, connects with the energy of the universe. Many times in the course of my ministry, I have heard people speak of saying their prayers in the morning or at night, but for me it is deeper than that. It is not just the words we fervently pray as we go to sleep, often asking for things, but it is how we live our lives in gratitude and thanksgiving. How we live our lives is a reflection of our prayers to the Creator. We may say thanks at night as we close our eyes but have we lived our thanks during the day, with each creature, each being that has crossed our paths?

Often I will find a little spider that has made her home in the corner of my kitchen ceiling. I ponder the tasks she has been given to do. It would be easy to just suck her into the vacuum as I do my cleaning. Instead, I carefully place her in a jar and release her outside.

I remind myself that when a cashier in the grocery store is grouchy and curt, another customer may have given her or him a difficult time. Maybe that person is worried about an ill child at home but can't afford to take the time from work to pay for medications. If I can take a couple of brief moments and give a smile or speak a soft word, maybe it can help change the rest of that person's day. I need to be *the prayer I bring to these wide miles of morning.*

The spirit of earth and wind is the same spirit that each of us carries within us. Yet sometimes it is we who think we are the greatest beings on earth. That's rather sad, for if all of human life disappeared, the rest of creation would heal itself. It is we who are pitiful creatures depending on all of creation.

I hope in some small way, I can be *true in passing.* It is not easy to live with integrity. It is not easy to know our own purpose for being and what it is that we are to fulfill while here for such a short time. One of our elders, Art Solomon, used to say that it is only the human race that has forgotten its duty and purpose. The tiny ants, the sun, the water and the moose all know theirs.

Qu'Appelle Valley

Jacqueline Bell

Crickets live here
in the bruised sage
yellowing green grass
         burning with wind

this is enough
it is more
and here always here

name these plants
their sounds: glottal, fricative, aspirant
huddle like tourists
         at the foot of this great beauty

sketches and photos are fumbling little parasites
on the back of this
         humped whale of otherness
that feet can track and track
and come no closer to

Black Owl

Susan E. McCaslin

I find you on the path,
flaccid mass of feather and bone,
cat ears laid back against your head,
eyes like wild broom, centres of daisies.

Your right wing is dusky as a raven's,
drooped like a broken wishbone.
I thrust you into my overcoat
and walk the long mile to wildlife refuge
praying all the zigzag way
into your luminous eyes.

On Moraine Hill

Nancy Mackenzie

this litany of my life
great plains words
horses run through my pastured dreams
kept rural and local
by so many section lines
well-sites, badger holes
the old rocks lichened
Indian tomahawk heads
white-tail and the black
coyote
songs of my sleep
great horned owl
binder twine about my feet

Inheritance

Debbie Voss

Growing up I remember playing often by the big oak trees that grew as a windbreak between the open fields of our farm and the sheltered yard. There I entered a magical new world where I heard birds flitting through the trees and sometimes caught sight of rabbits or partridges dodging through the undergrowth. There were so many layers of things for me to discover.

In the spring, melting snow ran off the fields through narrow channels carved into the soil. The rich, earthy smell of soil overwhelmed my senses. This was the time for walking through wet, newly revealed earth in squishing rubber boots, hearing the sucking sound as my feet were pulled down into mud pools until they merged and were held still for a moment. With great heaving I was usually able to free my encased feet, but there were moments of surprise when I couldn't, and the mire claimed more sacrificial boots for the season. It was in those moments that the humming, chilled earth bore forth the scent and sight of potential growth. I felt intimately connected with what *new life* meant in my world.

Once the soil started to dry out a bit, my dad and I did a *walk-about*, searching out large stones that could damage the machines, and seeing what treasures had risen to the surface during the winter's erosion. Every once in a while we found bottles, jars, even a watchcase discarded by someone in a previous generation. It was a small jump for me to imagine how people used these objects. Even now I have one of the cobalt jars I found, sitting on a shelf of my bookcase. It refracts the light of time through its coloured lens.

Summers shimmered off the heat of machines and people who tended the slowly ripening crops. In town my mom's vegetable garden ripened, too. While her corn stalks grew to hide the back fence, my father's wheat grew high and thick, its bearded stalks rippling in the wind. The late-setting sun cast a warm orange glow over everything and everyone. When I took off my shoes and walked barefoot through the earth, I still felt the heat stored from the day. The summer itself became a playmate whose blessings we were granted extended time to enjoy.

When fall arrived, time seemed to pass more quickly. Dad constantly checked the crops of wheat and flax to determine when it was time for thrashing and combining. Even with the ever-present pressure and exhaustion of ensuring that the harvest came in before the first bad frost, we still took the time to celebrate with family and friends at church and community fall suppers. These brought the sensory pleasures of homemade fruit pies and newly put up preserves. The women of the community bustled in the hall kitchen carrying platters laden with the fruits of their gardens and fields. Often there were fresh fall flowers cut and arranged amongst sheaves of grain to brighten the tables.

At these gatherings I heard bits of the stories of my parents and their families. I heard tales of one-room schoolhouses and of gathering eggs from stubborn hens, of bumper crops and the worry of storms, of years of lean picking but never going without. The spirit of the land resonated within the lives of these people and they gave thanks for it.

Fall makes me nostalgic, even now, for the summer that has just been. And as the geese leave and the leaves turn and fall and begin to crunch underneath my feet, I am reminded that we are entering a hallowed time. Autumn is a lesson in transition as the restful rhythm of nature offers us an example of the need to experience fallowness with all of creation.

Once the frost begins to appear more and more frequently on the trees and grass in beautiful lace-like patterns, I know that winter is well on its way. In southern Manitoba that can be anywhere from mid-October to early November, and while the date may always be in question, the inevitability of it is not. Winter brings with it an eerie stillness to our land. When the snow flies in earnest, I love to put on my *mukluks*, the product of the creative wisdom of our aboriginal people. In them I can crunch across the top of the wind-crested snow. Standing outside in the light of a full moon, seeing everything bathed in a cool, blue glow and hearing the wind's song in the stillness, I feel my soul's existence among the vast pattern of all creation. In that moment I can just be in a world that often crowds out this awareness. In that moment I feel the slow, deep pulse of the earth's heart and let it slow the pace of mine, as I draw deep cold breaths through the thick material of my bundled scarf and let that sparseness heal my busied soul. In that moment the land offers a balm. And with great awe and respect I accept it.

Crevice Prayers

Celeste N. Snowber

I find solace
  in crevices
  gray rocks
splattering beads
salt water
lapping skin.

Sunken shapes
  weathered rocks
  Goddess sofa
  calling my wet
  cold body
to bask
in its arms.

Enveloped
enfolded
  in strength
  ground rising
seaweed earth.

I too
  fold in
  as I drink sea
into thirsty skin.

I wrap
my body
in roughness.

Aged stone
grounds flesh
I pray
  through
my pores.

Earth/stone prayers
in waters of God.

Galiano Island   August 1998

Tankas

Claudia C. Morrison

I.
It was once believed
that trees were perfect yogis
willing to give up
the pleasures of travel, change,
newness: willing to sit still.

2.
A sudden squawking
beyond the treeline, reaching
crescendo overhead.
They pass: the stillness resumes,
like water after a wave.

Author's Note: The tanka is the ancestor of the seventeen syllable haiku. It consists of thirty-one syllables in a 5-7-5-7-7 pattern, and represents the distillation of an experience, one that usually takes place in a natural setting. Saigyo, a twelfth-century Buddhist monk, was a master of the form. His tankas captured experience in language that was direct and pared of anything superfluous. It has been a challenge for me to write these tankas in a way that is simple and yet resonant with many meanings.

Now Words, Years Later

Mary Gazetas

In this excerpt from a longer essay, the author writes of her experiences paddling the coast of British Columbia.

My paddling trips always heighten my senses. The sound of rain on my tent at night, winds hitting the trees first. I hear distant boats, voices. Whistle buoys out in the reefs, foghorns, ship's whistles. The noise of seals smacking up the water and the splash of a fish. Then fog muffles the sounds, distorts the distances.

Once, when I was busy on shore, my back to the beach and the open water, I heard three orcas breathing and swimming behind me. I turned and shouted "Look! Whales, over there, at four o'clock."

During a trip with my sister, we look for water, a stream we couldn't seem to find. We had to remind ourselves to stop, to listen. A running creek is often heard before it's seen. We look carefully and look again. Someone might have left a signal to the water's source: a rope, an old fishing float, something left behind to aid a thirsty paddler, running out of water.

Another time, I enter a dark Emily Carr forest, looking for eagle feathers to adorn our canoes and kayaks, to give us a safe journey. Spirits. Twisted trees and dense underbrush. I see animal trails, their lairs under stumps filled with fragments of bones. My sister's friends from the T'Sou-ke Band have taught her the custom of placing a clamshell in her kayak to keep her strong and safe. It was a Haida friend who taught us how to chant to the land and forest spirits—to ask permission to land our canoes and stay as guests. And when we leave, to always call out a special thank-you before paddling away.

We walk through the deserted village of Nuchatlitz, near Nootka Island. I stand in an overgrown baseball field filled with berries and wildflowers. In the grass is an old iron bedspring, a team's home bench. It is like a dream. I hear voices of children. But it is the voices of children on the beach with their families They have returned from their village up the inlet to harvest the plentiful shellfish.

One summer I paddle up in the Knight Inlet area. It is very different from the open blues, the exposed west coast of Vancouver Island. I am happy to be in a canoe again with my daughter Calliope and her dog, River. It has rained and the fog is descending. Great blankets of fog. A different kind of beauty. *Fogworks*—a new word to express what we enjoy. Suddenly we are in an area where the low tide exposes miles of thick, dark green seaweed, called nori. The sea's saltwater smells sweet and inviting. It is intoxicating, and everywhere. Eventually it gets into our hair, our clothes. When we return home, the stains and smells have been washed away.

Some of my favourite smells are the ones experienced on a hot sunny day: smells of pine and arbutus trees, reminding me of Howe Sound, near Vancouver, where I spent many childhood summers. Scents of summer-warmed woods carried out over the water by the breeze. Smells of the smoky wood fire, the first morning coffee, filling the air. These smells come first, before the sounds that signal the start of another new day.

My journals catch what I record on each paddling journey. Now I read these words again, years later. Words scribbled to help me remember the special places I have been. Hand drawn maps, recipes of what we cooked, lists of what we found. One year an inventory of fishing floats. Another year a list of wild flowers. Or a list of what to bring the next summer. How I felt after being storm-bound. One year there was a list of what people had said sitting around the fire. Our talk had shifted to menopause chats. Michael, my son, said after awhile, "for once in my life, I have absolutely nothing to say."

And always the pen and ink drawings of shells, stones, beaches, camp kitchens and rocks. These drawings fill the pages with impressions and memories. They come home with the stones, the smells and the stories as part of the sharing and passing of another coastal summer.

The People of the Deer Remembered

Gwen Molnar

Circled near a Barren's blaze,
Held in thrall by a shaman's gaze,
Ihalmiut* saw creation's dawn
When, as a cold north moon looked on,
All of the Tundra creatures came,
Chanting the magical, mystic names,
        Ka-i-la, Ka-i-la
        Hek-en-juk - juk
        Pa-i-ga, Wen-i-go
        Tak-tik - tuk.

Ptarmigan and a raven flock,
Snowy owl and rough-legged hawk,
Falcon, curlew and sea gulls came,
Chanting the magical, mystic names,
        Ka-i-la, Ka-i-la
        Hek-en-juk - juk
        Pa-i-ga, Wen-i-go
        Tak-tik - tuk.

Caribou and a musk ox pair,
Arctic fox and polar bear,
White wolf wild from the frozen plain,
Chanting the magical, mystic names,
        Ka-i-la, Ka-i-la
        Hek-en-juk - juk
        Pa-i-ga, Wen-i-go
        Tak-tik - tuk.

Wolverine and great brown bear,
Tundra vole and Arctic hare,
Lemming, weasels and ground squirrels came,
Chanting the magical, mystic names,
        Ka-i-la, Ka-i-la
        Hek-en-juk - juk
        Pa-i-ga, Wen-i-go
        Tak-tik - tuk.

* Ihalmiut - pronounced halmiut

Giant beast from polar seas,
Only known in memories,
With their small lake-cousins came,
Chanting the magical, mystic names,
   Ka-i-la, Ka-i-la
   Hek-en-juk - juk
   Pa-i-ga, Wen-i-go
   Tak-tik - tuk.

Summoned by the shaman's spell,
Each with ancient tales to tell,
Ihalmuit, beasts and fish and birds,
Found from one another's words
Their communal heritage,
From creation through each age,
Strong and sure the great refrain
Rose then as they called the names,
   Ka-i-la, Ka-i-la
   Hek-en-juk - juk
   Pa-i-ga, Wen-i-go
   Tak-tik - juk.

As the Ihalmiut joined the song,
As the shaman's drum beat on,
They relived enchanted nights,
When 'neath the dancing Northern Lights,
All of the Tundra creatures came,
Chanting the magical, mystic names,
   Ka-i-la, Ka-i-la
   Hek-en-juk - juk
   Pa-i-ga, Wen-i-go
   Tak-tik - juk.

Based on Farley Mowat's, **People of the Deer**

Arctic Theatre

Cathy Hodgson

It is nine at night. The town of Pine Point is quiet now. Window by window the lights go out. One more night in this borrowed town, this jagged edge of our landscape. No one really sleeps here. They just wait to go to work. Pass the time in dreaming until the next shift, the next and the next until it is time to go south, to go home.

The bunkhouse guys, as we call them, are gathering by threes and fours in their honeycomb cells where women are forbidden. They can lose their job in the mine and be sent home faster than you can say ptarmigan feather. They'll have one drink, then another, listening to Neil Young's *Heart of Gold* or Rod Stewart's *Maggie May* on the jukebox. Then stagger into their shift in the pits, or the crusher or the sump pumps the next morning.

We're in time capsules. Pre-fabricated houses with siding made of vinyl. Last summer a bear walked in from the bushes and tore off the corner of Burt's house just after wild strawberry season.

But this is January. The bears are sleeping. Not waiting for anything.

You can feel it before you see it—electricity in the air. Something pulls you out. The garbage you need to empty. The key you left in the ignition of the Ski-doo. Donning the shoes closest to the door, your brother's coat draped over your shoulders, you leave your little yellow squares of light.

You walk into an Arctic theatre with a sky you saw and smelled each night but forgot you were sensing. And there above Orion are poles of light beginning to dance. The dry wind is an organ pumping music only your blood can hear.

The cold burns your nose as you look up; tilt your face to the sky. You're pulled across the yard, the walk. You stand on the road. There are only two fences in this town—one for the superintendent and one for the Gibbon's Saint Bernard. Your tiny body marks the top of the town's circle. The air bites your nostrils with joy and your tears freeze in microscopic snowballs on the end of each lash.

These are goddesses leaping colours of spring—crimson and periwinkle and crocus bud green. They are laughing. They are bending and leaping. They rule the sky. They expand and shrink their rounded stage. They are Kali and Maya and Gaia. They have found me, pulled me into the steel dawn, the wild morning they've made of night.

They are my mentors. They say come dance the sky.

And I cry, I will. I will.

Juiced

Luanne Armstrong

Bees crawl drunk
out of fallen plums
or hang exhausted on the rank springing stalks
of sweet clover.
Wasps dance orbits around the last thickening grapes.
The lake is blue enough for heaven
and still warm for wading.
Tamaracks blaze
on the high places.

These days travel through my soul
like syrup,
call me out
to wander across a bright and misty landscape
dusted yellow,
where the sun-warmed reflection of pumpkins
wars with the dying light on the cedars
green and brown beadwork
tipping each branch.

Dizzy, struck over and over
by this gospel chorus
round and round
this wild buzzing
falling drunk from the centre
of the last peach.

꙳

II
The Land Remembers

On the backs of ancient seas I stand
among fallen mountains
The oldest stars within my hand
Long journey travelled

Trilogy - Ancient Seas
Carolyn McDade

Trilogy ~ Ancient Seas

On the back of an-cient seas I stand a - mong fall - en

moun - tains The old-est stars with - in my hand Long

jour - ney tra - veled Who goes the way ne - ver to

fall a - way? Who hon-ours faith - ful- ness more than o -

be- di - ence? Who trusts I make my path when I know not the way?

Trilogy - Ancient Seas

Carolyn McDade

On the back of ancient seas I stand
among fallen mountains
The oldest stars within my hand
Long journey traveled

Who goes the way
never to fall away?
Who honours faithfulness more than obedience?
Who trusts I make my path when I know not the way?

In wind the Old One flies
Wing shadow passing
The journey where all longings lie
O long migration

Who goes the way
never to fall away?
Who honours faithfulness more than obedience?
Who trusts I make my path when I know not the way?

Still the stars swing, wild with faith
Long passion burning
Who will come and take my place
New mountains rising

Who goes the way
never to fall away?
Who honours faithfulness more than obedience?
Who trusts I make my path when I know not the way?

At Kittiwake

Kerry Mulholland

here the moon is so bright
undiluted starlight has spilled on my lashes
tickled them open
here there is an echo of evening coyote
trembling my bones awake

and this sky

this sky so close it crept through the window
lifted me from the cradle of a downy bed
to set me beneath its unfurling

this sky is rocking me dazzled
and the stars spin their passage overhead

it is so very silent

I can hear the earth arching her back
to meet the sky

I can hear ancestor bones a mile away
hear them joining with the soil
beside the old white church

beneath the curved arm of this night

I want to lie on the ground
belly to earth and hang on
arms outstretched and fingertips reaching
cling like an infant to this mother
suckled by gravity
held fast in the gaze
of the moon's bright eye

The Taste of Memories

Kelsey Andrews

The trees whisper greetings as I pass
and wave to me in the wind
the mud is spongy
on the road where I walk.
Along the way I pick a few saskatoons -
they're always sweeter
beside their bush-mothers,
as if they still remember
their days as baby berries
nourished by their umbilical twigs
and rocked by the wind
tickled under their chins
by young blue spruce
while the matronly aspens
look on and murmur.
As if the sweetness of their memories
can still be tasted in their flesh.

Divining

Shirley A. Serviss

If I were a diviner,
I would walk this province,
wand of willow in my hand,
watch it wave like prairie grass
or wind in whispering aspen,
point me to artesian
currents of women's history
I know flow just beneath
the surface, find graves
of babies they birthed
alone and couldn't save,
divine the sacred places
where their secret hopes
and fears are buried,
witch wells they filled
with lonely tears.

the tipi ring

Doris Bircham

in a quiet moment I am drawn
inside a ring of stones
half-buried in the earth
where no plough has touched
a knoll where blue gramma grass
sage and nodding wild onion
hold tight to the sod

buffalo wallows dent the slopes
at the foot of a willow
a spring bubbles up from the ground
rushes over cobblestones

have chokecherries always
sun-ripened as they do now
in the coulee
have the horned larks been first
to circle the skies in spring
while curlews pierce the sloughs
with their sickle-bills

some rocks are laced with lichen
when I lean back and close my eyes
I can almost smell smoke
from a campfire
I put my ear close to the ground
imagine I hear the wind
rustle the leather skirt
of a Cree woman
her moccasins
whisper through tall grass
as she walks toward
the circle of stones

The Grub-Box Quilt

Willow Barton

I dedicate this story to the Peoples of the Land. The stories we tell of life and of the living of life are often unwritten and unpublished.

We were poor. That much is true. There were the trips to the second hand stores and the sometimes hand-me-downs. There is no bitter-sweetness attached to being poor.

Many have been here. It is Canada—the stuff of dreams and fabric remade and of the memories of sky and land. It is about patterns and things made of symmetrical balance, things that laid roots in the Alberta and Saskatchewan soils where buffalo grasses and long-stemmed red grasses once rippled. It is the story of the us and the we and the *sometimes* intermingling.

***

Mom can count to ten on her fingers and then backtrack, add on. Though she wants my sister and me to figure on paper, she still apologizes for the leaving.

In the convent, days pass slowly into months. "How many until we go home?" My sister Bernadette who is older writes it down. "This many."

In summers, we weave our way across Alberta and Saskatchewan, stooking and rock-picking. Even before we finish at one farm the talk begins of finding work elsewhere. Ahead is the open road. There are prairie elevators; burnt-umber and fire-red and ten feet tall. Sometimes the walls are painted with the favorite disciples—Matthew, Mark, Luke or John and these painted with God's words upon them.

When it comes to the Bible, Mom can read most words and knows some verses. Sometimes she reads by the kerosene lamp. She also knows how to make us laugh. With her hands together she makes shadows of geese with wings that open wide and a wolf that yawns lazily. We do not watch her hands but only the shadow animals that come to life. She knows how to make these things. Other things, she cannot know.

She looks up across the land as we travel. Of the remaining sod houses beneath a hill: she says, "Some lived this way beneath the earth, dug out houses and they lived." Other houses are above ground. Some are log and others red-tar papered with black roofs. Sometimes the doors are half-unhinged and the walls still standing surround a gaping hole that frames the expanse of sky.

Tumbleweeds sit in corners until a stronger wind comes along. We are like these, always moving but always returning to my mother's reserve. It is the small patch of land that holds us firm between times.

On the reserve, though, there is little work. But we have refined moving to an art. There are sooty pans and an axe; there is a full canvas tent neatly folded, some plastic and olive-coloured army blankets. Mom's patchwork quilt, still on-going, is wrapped around a tin of fabric scraps. There is the grub-box and the white enamel plates and a kerosene lamp.

By Waseka we work for a farmer. His house is set neatly upon the land. His wife though, is ill and can't work long hours. For a few dollars per month Mom cleans house for the Mrs.

One day Mom comes into the house where we are living and she says, "The Mrs. is coming to visit." There is silence except for the bluebottle fly's occasional buzz at the window. It is only mid-morning but already the day is warm.

"We were polishing silver and talking quilts. I do not know." Mom pauses as she looks off into space. "It's not as if it is fancy or anything." But she smiles taking out the ironing cloths, for she does not often have the company of women her age. Once pressed, the quilt is given the extra chair at the table.

Then the Mrs. is at the door. Her dress is blue and it has little red flowers. She looks too young to be a Mrs.

After tea, she turns. "This is the quilt then? It is interesting but you could cut the squares the same size. It has nice colours, though it needs composition."

"I am still adding to it." Mom is measuring, too. She has met all kinds of Mrs. across the land. There are big-boned women who can stook alongside their men and then turn out a good quilt. And yet size is not everything. There are others, smaller women with wills of iron who can wield an axe or a needle equally well.

It is more than the neat stitches that make a quilt. It is the knowing; it is what one does with what one has. Little remainders of the scraps that are not wasted but put away toward the making of a future quilt. It is more than even squares.

Beads have gathered in the small space above Mom's mouth. Small water drops glisten on her bronze skin. The day is made warmer by the iron cooling on the stove.

Between sips of tea the Mrs. says, "Yes. I can see that you are still working on it." There is no more talk about the quilt and the awkwardness has passed. Soon they are telling about this one or that one and some of the crazy things that have happened.

Some stories are true and others, who knows? Things have been added in the telling. Mom tells the story about a man at the Biggar hotel who fell into the outhouse hole. The man who found him, upon hearing the voice calling up from the darkness, "Is there anybody up there?" almost had a heart attack.

Nobody could be found to pull out the poor guy below. They finally got somebody with a rig and the poor guy was pulled out. He was walking stone sober beside the rig when the wheel ran over his foot. It was forty degrees below outside and at the hospital they wouldn't let him in until they hosed him down.

"It was that way alright," says the Mrs. "And it is a darn good thing we could laugh in spite of it all. We knew we had to continue and what had to be done. Is that not so? When my own mother came from Montreal, it was her sewing box, the paper patterns, needles and thread; those were most important."

The Mrs. puts her cup down. "On-going work. We continue with a work until it is finished to the best of our abilities, until it is *fini'*, no more to add and no more to take away."

"Ahh. I think I understand what you mean. It is a thing done, yes?" Mom stresses the *Yes*.

"You understand then." The woman smiles and seems pleased. After tea she shakes Mom's hand and thanks her. "It is a good quilt."

***

Later Mom tells us about trading. "All peoples, they trade when they talk about the way one does things or the other does things. We already traded things with others before the *Mooniyow*[1] came. And when they came, we traded with them too.

"The Cree women used to make quill work on moccasins and things. It was not like work because we always laughed lots when we women worked together. And we made nice things—nice roses on vests we made with quills. But when the churches came, the women saw the kinds of embroidery on the priests' vests and the table cloths. They had roses with two colours and the curving lines of the vine-work and leaves. The women they saw these things. Then at home they made these designs into beadwork using two colours also.

"We always traded. Before the white people came, us that are the Peoples of the Land, we traded blue clay and other things; sometimes a little copper from way up north or with others we traded shells. When the *Mooniyow* brought glass beads, we never saw or knew anything like this. Mamask![2] This glass that was capturing the light. And our men traded so we could have these beads and other things."

Mom shrugs her shoulders slightly. "Yesterday or today . . . sometimes there are designs that people change, but people stay the same. I think so. But some things can change, like the land. It can change. It is a living thing, what we call our mother, this earth, because it gives us life."

This is a time when red-orange tiger lilies spill across forests and down coulee ditches. Who wouldn't think this would last forever? The orange flash of a Baltimore Oriole's wing is missed if one doesn't look up quickly.

---

[1] *Mooniyow* refers to the first white people that came. *Mooniyow* rhymes with *Sooniyow* which means money. It may be that the Cree word came from trading with those that had first coins, then in later years, paper money.
[2] In Cree, *Mamask* is strange or wonderful.

After the work is done, there is the repacking again of those things we have used and those that are there in case—the plastic and the tent. But these are the most important things: the family held together and the keeping up of house and home in transit. And always the land as we search the next horizon.

Our Dad doesn't speak much about the farm he's left behind him, his land or his legal wife. There is that too. He does not speak of his own Sioux grandfather as freely as our Mother speaks of her people. But he knows the way of making strong fence posts and he knows of the water that bubbles beneath the rocks. He says things once and expects us to remember. So in peeling the daily-rationed oranges from the grub-box, we no longer ask the why of the lock on the grub-box. "Because if the oranges are all eaten today, and at one time, they are gone and there is none for tomorrow."

He never forgets things. Christmas one time, we came home. The night before Christmas it is very cold. Looking for socks beneath our bed, my sister and I find a box of Mandarin oranges. We celebrate our good luck to the last orange before we sleep.

After this when there is fruit in the grub-box, the lock is on it.

There are the things we have no experience of. "What was it like?" We have an endless supply of questions. And in their answers, our parents do not underline the learning; there is no capital E on education. And then "tell me" follows the discovery of old newspaper in the attic and the joists behind the white-clayed walls.

"What was it like to live in *your* time, and tell us about the war and things." We do not know much about the war except that Dad's flat feet stopped him marching off to it.

So he speaks of war—a man's viewpoint, adding on where Mom has no understanding. "The things we fight for," he says. "Our land and to be free and to be held as people, our beliefs and our rights held as real as any citizen of this country."

And this so we will know the *whys* in later years; why people deprived of luxury save tiny bits of string wound into balls and scavenge rusty nails that they'll never use. All the *whys* of the land and simply this: "The way it was . . . there was this land. It came that many saw it was rich and good and the things that grew on it. Turnips and cabbage were big. Bigger than a man's hand and encircling it four times. No wonder it was a hunger. It is a hunger that will always be. The hunger for this soil: that is why people came here and still come. It gets into the blood; the smells of earth that is alive." These are our Dad's words.

And we have more questions. The *why*: why do we travel? And the *how come*: the how come of others and their neat, picket fences? "Because it just is." There is no debating. It is just a fact of life. Our parents' labour shields us and allows us our innocence.

For fun and a quarter for each smaller rock picked, my sister and I work the fields. And there is Dad and Mom levering boulders that God has put down some time before and we kids are arguing the chance that we have found gold in this rock or another. The time, too, our parents speak in hushed tones, things we are not supposed to hear.

All summer my sister and I have been stringing together our parents' words from fragments that the wind brings, trying to figure together the puzzles of childhood. At summer's end and just before we leave for school, there is Mom crying at the leaving. She stands again in that far-off field until Dad has to go and get her. We are made wise about rocks and about the giving up of a life too soon.

Then we are leaving. The names of towns we pass are fleeting sounds upon our tongues.

***

Our Mom speaks. "It was a long time ago." She chooses her words carefully. She speaks in English and very slowly. "It was a time before when the earth on the plains dried up and blew away. This was the time I was born in the Thirties. The old ones they speak of this. What it was and why it was this way, who knew?"

She says, "I have learned from your Dad about farming. Myself though, I do not believe in things that are perfect. There is no such thing as perfect. And there should be a place for animals and natural things. The way it was intended by the Creator."

She traces her hands across the quilt she has been working on, then holds them together. "A long time ago, the earth was full of life and other people came here. Even on your Dad's side, they came crossing by Montana. It was the land and the rivers and they came from all over. We Cree understood this hunger to be with the land and of the land, though we saw it was different, this kind of hunger that others had, because they had to own the papers on the land."

Her hands unfold. "I have known the passing of time. There were the many sloughs that the ducks and other water birds lived in. And our people gathered wild eggs. One time there were many kinds we ate, even wild quail eggs. And we had wild pheasant that foraged among the coulees. This was where the willows with roots kept in the water. There were other kinds of plants too, with smaller roots that held water to the earth.

"What happened in the thirties, the old ones wondered about and they did not know, either. In other years, the rain came steady. Always it came at some time. Beginning in 1915 and into the thirties when I was born. My own mother told me it was different in her time before this.

"But the rain, for a long time, didn't come so much. Winds came instead. By that time there were not so many willow bluffs to catch the little rain that fell or to even trap the wind. And there were fewer birds. The wind's song though, it came, whistling across open prairies and flat lands, and carrying the earth's soil with it. When the grasshoppers came there were fewer birds to eat them. The people kept on planting but the grasshoppers ate trees and wheat the same. Nobody could tie it into one thing to explain it."

Her hands are again upon the quilt. "There is this. No straight lines on my quilt." She points to the cross-stitching and the uneven patches. "See, there is no one way to do things because there is no such thing as the perfect way. Just like that I wished I could have gone further in school. Maybe then I would see the way of ordering things and on paper too. But I know this. You cannot take everything off the land. Not without the leaving of some things for life and for the animals too."

She speaks the last sentence so quietly that Dad turns. There is a look on his face, as if he thinks that he should say something, add a few words. He says nothing.

***

It is Mom's words that linger over the years. Her quilt is fading now, the edges of its boundaries frayed. Only the colours make each section stand out distinctly. Some pieces are as brown as my skin—brown as the place that I am from, the rich clay earth I am born to and which someday I will return to. There my bones will be the dentine of new rock and my ashes the stuff of new silt.

There are those who will tell their stories of the birthing and dying and of the laughter in between. Others will write of hardship and heroism or about those who shaped history with text. A rock chipped away here or there will undoubtedly leave greater monuments that record these people's passing.

The wind is a great equalizer—the wind that blows over W.O. Mitchell's script and over those Saskatchewan things he wrote of so beautifully, the transient things that in passing are taken into the land again.[1]

As far as the history that threads me so certainly to my people and to the past and tomorrow, we are the Cree. In the river of language, in our words, our memories are carried forward. We too, record and bring forward a time passed and some things gone: those wild flowers like crocus hills, that some humans have never seen and will never see, the shifting syllables of purple or emerald and sap green. These are the tracings of another time and place that we thread forward.

I have two things that are reminders of our dad and our mom. Of our Dad I have a grub-box. He did not say whether or not he made it and I do not know how it was brought here, if it crossed mountains or plains. But there are marks of a journey, of someone's hand upon the wood. The planed surfaces are down-cut, evidence a blade has passed here or there. It is a symmetrical box and has neat corners. Of my Mom I have a patchwork quilt. It is made with uneven squares. These are seemingly put together without rhyme or reason. In places there are unintentional patterns, these patches faded by yellow sunlight falling. But it is the quilt that really captures the sense of what is important. It is always the land that came before us and continues after us. And in the rivers of language that flow, these carry our words backwards and forwards, so we will know. *Ekosi-Maka*.[2]

[1] W.O. Mitchell. Who Has Seen the Wind? Toronto: MacMillan Canada, 1947. Mitchell quotes Psalms ciii: 15 - 16, "As for man, his days are as grass: as a flower of the field, so he flourisheth. For the wind passeth over it, and it is gone: and the place thereof shall it know no more.
[2] Ekosi-Maka. That is all. There is no more to say.

Dustbowl Dreams

Candace Duiker

I remember
your dear calloused hands, steeped in sweetness.
Keepers of love and givers of life.
The hot winds blew but never broke you.
Dead soil danced itself alive again,
then rolled into the dust bowl of forever.
Still you stood.
Granny, your rose-water hugs
made it okay again.
I know, I know,
I can hear you now:
rivers are born from cracks in the earth's
navel

Cut Stalks in Her Arms

Mary Maxwell

We bury Grandfather in late November in the cemetery near Plenty,
Saskatchewan. Aunt Lily asks for no flowers at his funeral   only dried
wheat stalks please—Bearded Durham/No.l Hard/Marquis tied
together with rust coloured ribbon   tearing in the wind

An orphan now, my father releases a handful of clay   a prayer
requiem pace

After the funeral, in the city flower shop, stalks of freesia, the petals
cool   rows of tight blossoms open into throats slender & fragile
my face in their fragrance

A memory:

My grandmother in her garden, walking among rows and rows
blossoms   the colours wild against the shelterbelt of trees   visited
them twice daily, morning and evening fed and watered   trimmed and
pruned   cradled the cut stalks in her arms like children

Making Our Way by Heart:
Reflections on Women-Land-Spirt, a Sacred Web

Ruth Blaser

Judy Delorme

Qu'Apelle Valley, Saskatchewan

One summer afternoon when I was a young woman in my late twenties Donna Pinay, a Cree woman and I, together walked the land my grandparents settled in the early 1900s. Donna and I sat at the fire circle near Buffalo Rock, visited and ate. As the sun was setting Donna said to me, "You know Ruth, before this land was your people's it was my people's." In the acknowledgement of this truth, and the painful history of domination of First Nations people and land, we two young and idealistic women with such rocky and harsh historical terrain between us decided that we would rename these hills and coulees that are so much a part of both our stories. According to the rural municipality map, the official name of this place is *Loon Creek*. But on that day Donna and I renamed it *Grandmothers Hills* for all grandmothers, all ancient and wise ones who care for life.

Nearly three years ago at the time of the Harvest Moon, a group of women from Western Canada came together with Carolyn McDade at Prairie Christian Training Center in Ft. Qu'Appelle to dream and sing a new project into being. We had chartered a bus to take us to Grandmothers Hills so we could walk together there on unbroken ground. However, quirky prairie weather brought a storm of heavy wet snow on that Thanksgiving afternoon, so we adjusted our plans. Rather than trying to make our way across country roads we opted for a trip on *hard top* around the Calling Lakes of the Qu'Appelle Valley.

From Periwinkle we drove further on the impossibly narrow road to B-say-tah Beach. Neither bus driver nor guide knew exactly where we were going. At that time Judy Delorme, a Cree woman from Fisher River who now lives in Winnipeg, asked if we might go to Lebret and the place of the former Indian Residential School. So we made our way along the north side of Mission Lake, and then drove down the hill into Lebret. We passed the old fieldstone Sacred Heart Church on Main Street and drove on to the site of the school. Judy had been a student at Birtle, Manitoba and not at the Lebret School, but being on this land still placed her in the story of her family. As we approached, there was a great and sudden stirring of our hearts.

Here is Judy's story.

There we were in front of the school. I was startled. I wasn't expecting to be there. When we were suddenly there I thought, I'll tell you my story of Women-Land-Spirit. All of the schools were really the same in the way they were built and the way they were run. I was not at this school, but one just like this one.

As a little girl I lived with my grandparents at Fisher River. My grandmother died when I was nine. Just a week after she died we were taken to school. My uncle, who was like a brother to me, and I were taken. My uncle was fourteen. I was nine. He spoke Cree. He couldn't speak English.

I can still see my grandfather standing in the garden while we were leaving.

I was not physically or sexually abused at residential school. My pain from residential school was more like my whole family's pain. My grandfather was blind. After my grandmother died and we were taken he was alone. Leaving him there still really hurts me. We needed each other.

Coming away from Fisher River, losing my grandmother, leaving my grandfather . . . My uncle eventually ran away and he has never had a home to this day.

I used to sleep with my grandmother. My grandfather slept in a little single bed in our small house and I slept with my grandmother, at her back. I went from the security of sleeping at my grandmother's back, to residential school.

When I got there, the other girls had already been there for a few months. They seemed adjusted. After I thought everyone was sleeping, I would allow myself to cry.

I was feeling really lonely that night. Then I felt my grandmother's back at my back. I felt her back at my back in this strange land. After that I felt stronger. I didn't feel so lonely after that. My grandmother came to me that night. I realize it was my grandmother's spirit that has carried me to this day.

*This is my story of Women-Land-Spirit. I share my story
because I want people to know. It wasn't just those who
went to residential school who suffered. It was our whole
family. If they'd left Colin, my uncle, at home, Grandfather
might have been able to stay.*

*They brought us from our life—we had a garden, a cow,
chickens, eggs. Our people were self-sufficient. They
brought us from our life."*

As Judy spoke that cold, snowy Thanksgiving afternoon, we listened,
bearing witness to what she remembered and to what the land
remembered. We listened and we wept. In that moment we became a
sacred web of women, sitting in the bus together, then huddled and
weeping in a place where people and land have known sorrow, healing,
shame and restoration.

Some seasons later, during the Circle of Relations Summer Gathering
in August 2000, our hope and intention was once again to walk
Grandmothers Hills. This time the weather cooperated. Thirty women
and two girls traveled the dusty roads on the north side of the
Qu'Appelle valley and made our way there. We left our vehicles
parked in a long raggedy line in the ditch, then walked first through a
field of lentils and peas nearly ready to be swathed, then through a
barbed wire gate and onto the unbroken land. I love to watch women
walk on land, moving slowly, talking, calling to one another as some
move together while others find their own path. I love what stirs in
our hearts as we make our way. So on that particular August day my
heart was full.

Toward dusk, we eventually gathered around the fire circle at Buffalo
Rock. This ancient and great stone presence rises out of the hillside
like a buffalo welcoming the sunrise. The girls climbed their wonderful
little girl bodies all over the old-old rock, singing and calling and
pointing toward the great open valley. Some women walked the
coulees while others sat. Grace, one of the crones, placed her chair
close to it and sat there looking out into the valley from the time of
our arriving until dark. As sunset came we sat together in silence,
listening. Then some took their leave while others stayed to welcome
the dark. The stars shone with a clear brilliance on that August night.
There were long sighs and quiet conversations. Then too soon, the
mosquitoes came. We reluctantly put out the fire and made our way

through the warm calm darkness to our cars. I can still feel my joy at walking hand in hand in hand, not seeing the path, not seeing the gopher holes or the cow pies, not even seeing my own feet. That night we made our way, as we do so often in this movement, not by sight but by heart, leaning into the goodness of life and the ever unfolding meanings of *Women-Land-Spirit: a Sacred Web*. There was a growing sense that we had become a tribe, gathering in circles to sing, reflect and give creative and artistic expression to our passion and compassion for all life, then scattering to be leaven in our homelands.

In recent years as I walk this land with women, I am coming to know it as land that holds joy and healing, that holds and respects broken and joyful hearts. Its vastness calls forth imagination and visions. It enables hearts of discernment and embraces hearts of gratitude. But I am also coming to know this land as vulnerable. Racism is deeply planted in the social fabric that surrounds it. Hard feelings, misunderstanding, ignorance and harsh judgments run deep between "white settlers" and Aboriginal people.

These words were spoken by a Crow elder at a conference of Native American leaders and activists in Bozeman, Montana in the mid-seventies. "You know, I think if people stay somewhere long enough—even white people—the spirits will begin to speak to them. It's the power of the spirits coming up from the land. The spirits and the old powers aren't lost, they just need people to be around long enough and the spirits will begin to influence them."[1] My own sense is that some day Grandmothers Hills will be returned to Donna Pinay's people, and that will be a good thing.

---

[1] Sharon Butala. *Wild Stone Heart, An Apprentice in the Fields.* Toronto: Harper Flamingo Canada, 2000, p. 188.

Grandmother's Land

Bernadette L. Wagner

Rolling hills like Grandmother's curves
comfort me take me home to my self
to where I am born and reborn.

Covered with crocuses and gray-green wool
this land speaks, lulls me
as Grandmother's *kleine* kind
sharp accent of sage fills me.

Trees green and full whisper
stories of the ancients as we wander a path
over boughs and burrows between poplar
and willow under dappled light and leaves.

As birds chirrup overhead Grandmother pulls me
close to an elm where young robins squeak
excitement as they feed.

A broken patch grows rows of beans and peas potatoes
and corn, radishes and onions at one end
three stands of rhubarb await pies raspberries
redden for jam and crabapples sweeten to juice.

Grandmother's house fills with the scent
of her magic when snow rests her land
backroom bees make quilts that warm me.

On Grandmother's land the seasons
follow one another. No matter what
the land will remember.

❧

III
Breaking the Web

All that comes,
to fall before its time.
All that breaks
the sacred web that binds.

Hills of Grass
Carolyn McDade

Hills of Grass

© 1995 by Carolyn McDade

O Liv-ing Land Spi - rit who sing-ing sang the hills Breath-ing the

sun and the rain spun a sa - cred Web The bro-ken and un-bro-ken of the

land the bro-ken and un-bro-ken of my life The times I reach, the

times that I re-frain The fur-row and fal-low turn-ing in the rain Come as the

grass comes Go as grass-es go The shin-ing hills of grass live on for

all that ris- es from these hills shall some day there re- turn a - gain

Hills of Grass

Carolyn McDade

O Living Land
Spirit who singing sang the hills -
Breathing the sun and the rain,
spun a sacred Web
The broken and unbroken of the land
The broken and unbroken of my life
The times I reach, The times that I refrain -
furrow and fallow turning in the rain
Come as the grass comes
Go as grasses go
The shining hills of grass live on
for all that rises from these hills
shall some day there return again

O Blessed Land
Hills rising haunted and serene
Long is the witness you've seen -
Fury and grace
All that comes, to fall before its time
All that breaks the sacred web that binds
By all we know, by all that we are known -
By all that is, and none can ever own
Come as the grass comes
Go as grasses go
The shining hills of grass live on
for all that falls into these hills
shall some way turn and rise again

We of the land -
Breathing and breathless of the hills -
move in the street and the field
hope of the land
The turning of green through shades of gold
Through all the shades of faith a life can hold
As wings of night unfold the wings of dawn,
within this day tomorrow spirals on
Come as the grass comes
Go as grasses go
The shining hills of grass live on
for all allying with this land
arise and sing tomorrow's hills

Hills of Grass: A Meditation

Ingrid Alesich

As a child, I spent an abundance of time with *living* land. When I was five years old, the youngest of four children, my mother died. After that, I chose the path by the stream in the woods to get to school. I imagined that the sacredness of Mother was embedded in the spirit of the forest, in every part of nature. It was a great source of strength and wonder for me.

A decade ago, I experienced another heavy loss of loved ones. I entered a long and painful journey of separation from the land. I yearned for that sense of connection I knew as a child.

Then this song, this poetry of the soul, *Hills of Grass*, gave me a new rich perspective. The hills, carved by glaciers millennia ago, still stand *haunted and serene* and as they erode new ones will be created. The mystery of this connection, this deep bonding of the ancient rhythms of nature, broadens my understanding of the webbing in our lives. Friends, family, community, living, dead, and not yet born, are woven into a sacred web.

I have grieved, fought and struggled against the scarring and polluting of this land, this planet. Yet, in the shadow of potential ecological disaster, this song assures me that the ancient hills of grass will live on. At the centre of this song is the compassion for, and the honouring of all life over universal time. Each time I hear or sing this song, I feel blessed by its healing power.

Hills of Grass: The Dance

Barb Yussack

Called in Spirit: *Rainbows Dancing Deer Woman*

I love to sing with Carolyn McDade and to spiritually experience her music. I also love to dance. For over a decade I have been a sacred circle Dancer—instructing, creating and always eager to learn new dances. Of the songs Carolyn McDade has written for the Canadian landscape, *Hills of Grass* is the one that affected me most deeply. It connects the dance between women, spirit and the land. I approached Carolyn about choreographing a sacred circle dance to one of her songs. She encouraged me to do so, and chose Hills of Grass as her personal preference. The new work quickly danced into existence. It reverences the land, weaving the threads of movement to those of sound in the great dance of life. Each movement and step is symbolically significant, transforming the song into physical prayer.

The dance begins with the sighing of the wind as dancers absorb in silence the gently blowing breeze of sound. The wind increases in intensity, and the dancers begin to travel, reflecting the clouds moving across the sky. The singing begins. The dancers pay homage to the land, bowing in respect and honouring Mother Earth. They begin to walk upon this sacred living land, and spin outwards, casting webs out into the universe. They remember the tiny creatures scurrying about, weaving their way through the grasses that are their homes. The dancers *come as the grass comes, and go as grasses go*, rooted in the earth, waving their stalks and stems in the wind. They gently step *on the back of ancient seas* to honour this gift, the eternal presence of the land.

The pattern repeats, its sedate movement a testament to the majesty and grandeur of the prairies and the hills. The clouds return, carried on the wings of the wind. The dance culminates in a vision of the grasses and grains of the prairies—the weeds, the wildflowers, the spidery fronds of the mosses, swaying in the breeze, giving thanks to this blessed land that gives of itself endlessly.

What I have left is imagining

Heather MacLeod

I used to live in the arctic,
but I left so often my leaving
became unnoticed, an event
which slipped away without celebration.

I used to live in the arctic,
thought I was a boomerang,
my point of origin the north,
but I grew up here in the Cariboo
with bit and bridle, Bay and Appaloosa,
instead of inukshuk and ulu, char and whitefish.

I used to live in the arctic,
found my ancestors' footsteps in the Northwest Passage
trailing behind Franklin and found
what it meant for me to be Metis.

I used to live in the arctic,
a place where my Indian blood
found room to live, elliptical
it moved within me, solid as packed snow,
smooth and clear as the first layer of ice
over the waters of Great Slave.

I used to live in the arctic,
and what I have left is imagining;
imagine me talking to you
frost trailing out with my breath;
pretend I speak sounds in the shape of syllabics,
say thank you in Dogrib, pretend I cry in Cree.

roadkill

Wynne Edwards

I am already losing the imprint of you I need some gesture a written
epitaph to hold you with me as you were at the Obed Summit lying
on that highway dignified stately limbs still the only movement your
frosty breath entering and re-entering the night air your brown eyes
meeting my brown eyes full of not fear what was it sorrow your
calf sent off by dying moose mother words be careful crossing the
highway I love you forever into dark night with nothing beyond our
headlights' reach me leaving you there to go to the humans covered
with glass getting colder he trapped in his minivan with one arm
broken she pacing anxious at the side of the road shaking glass
from her coat her hair spitting it from her mouth then rescue trucks
ambulances police cars seventeen workers with back boards flashing
lights stretchers the woman calming in the warmth of our car when I
return to you your breath has stopped you have died quietly without
support away from the white lights the jaws of life the woman
shouting I want that moose for my freezer

My Utopia

p k chamberlain

I trudge through the powdery snow. It sifts over the tops of my boots and settles around my ankles, melting then re-freezing to form icy socks. My sister trails behind me, swearing as she stumbles over hidden rocks. She is becoming impatient. I keep searching.

At first, we'd just wanted to get out of the hot, stuffy house to get some fresh air and burn off some Christmas-dinner calories. We wandered around the farmyard, looking at the cattle and pigs in their pens. Then I got the idea to look for my hut. So now we flounder in the deep snow in the north bush, around the old slough-bed, and into the willows behind it.

I look for the clearing. We weave through the willows, searching. All the trees look the same. Where is it? My mind slips back ten years as I try to remember.

***

When I was thirteen I decided to run away from home. I packed a bag full of clothes and books and put it in the back of my closet, ready for a quick escape. I knew that since I had no money, I'd have to stay close to home to steal food and supplies. I needed my own house, though. Images from *Island of the Blue Dolphins* and *My Side of the Mountain* churned through my head, but I didn't have Karana's whale ribs or Sam Gribley's giant tree. Finally I decided to build a hut out of scraps from my father's lumber pile.

For several days I hunted for the perfect place for my new home. Then I found it: a clearing in the willow trees on the edge of a slough about a quarter of a mile from my parents' house. A small, low opening in the bush formed the only entrance to the clearing. Not only was it practical, concealed by the dense, leafy willows that surrounded it, but it was also beautiful. The ground was carpeted with grass. The sun shone through the circle of trees to create a warm little pocket separated from the rest of the world. I spent several days getting to know the area and my clearing. I lay on the grass in the sun, staring into the blue sky and listening to the songs of birds that would perch in the branches above me if only I stayed still long enough. Frogs announced the approach of dusk with choruses of throaty chants. It was an ideal spot.

I decided that the first thing to do was to plant a garden. Then by the time my hut was finished, I would have food ready to eat. I smuggled a spade from Mom's shed and started to dig up a small section of the clearing. It wasn't as easy as I had thought it would be; underneath the grass, the ground was rocky and webbed with tough roots. It was difficult to get the shovel in more than a few inches. The soil came up in rock-like little chips, not at all like the velvety black gardens Mom kept. I knew that it would work, though. I meticulously planted stolen seeds of flowers and my favourite vegetables in neat rows: calendulas, potatoes, carrots, peas, corn. No broccoli or spinach or asparagus for me! I would be a free person and I'd eat what I wanted.

Next I built the fireplace. That was relatively easy. I scraped a shallow pit in the earth and lined it with flat rocks, four to form the sides and one on top to protect my fires from rain and snow. I collected dead branches and sorted them into piles for kindling and firewood under the umbrella of a willow. I was so proud of my beautiful fireplace. I lit a fire in it every time I went to the clearing.

Finally, I was ready to start work on the hut. I didn't need anything fancy—just a plain shelter to keep me dry and safe. I decided it would have to be up on stilts in case the slough ever flooded. It would be four feet by six feet—just big enough for me to sleep in—and four feet high—just tall enough for me to sit up in. There would be shelves all around the inside to hold clothes, food, and books.

At home, I patiently waited for Dad to leave for the fields. As soon as he was out of sight, I sneaked into the shop to gather the things I needed: a sledgehammer, a crowbar, and a metal five-gallon pail. I chose four sturdy posts from the lumber pile. I made several trips each day to drag supplies out to my clearing.

***

Mr. Johnson gave us a language arts assignment. We were to write an essay titled *My Utopia*. We were to imagine and describe our perfect world. I was so excited. Finally an assignment in which I could write whatever I wanted! Of course, I knew exactly what I would write about. So I described my hut on paper in meticulous detail, complete with dimensions and decorations, imagining how perfect it would be when it was finished. I told about my garden full of delicious vegetables and my fireplace with its comforting fire. The only thing I left out was the hut's location. I wrote about how I would live alone and do what I wanted, staying up until midnight every night to roast marshmallows and listen to the night songs of the animals.

I wrote and rewrote my essay. It had to be perfect. I was so proud of my hut and I wanted everyone to know about it. Wouldn't they be jealous when they found out I was really going to live there? Wouldn't they envy me because my utopia was real? I handed in the essay, knowing it was the best thing I had ever written.

•••

Meanwhile I struggled to build my hut. First I tried to make postholes with the crowbar. I wasn't strong enough to break very far through the dry soil. After many attempts I'd be left with only a small dent in the ground. Then I carefully balanced a post in the little hole, piling dirt around it to hold it upright. I stood on top of the upside-down five-gallon pail. Then, precariously balanced on my perch, I tried to lift the sledgehammer. It was very heavy. Sometimes I fell off the pail just trying to lift it. When I finally had the hammer hoisted up over the post and tried to take a swing, often I missed my target and the momentum of the hammer toppled me off the pail again. Sometimes the post fell and I'd have to start all over. When I did make contact, the vibrations of the impact shooting up the handle stung my hands. The post barely budged.

It was taking so long to drive the posts in I was getting frustrated. The work was much harder than I had expected. Each day it became more of an effort. I pounded and pounded on the stubborn posts, but they didn't move. Even when I piled dirt and rocks around them for support, the posts still wobbled. How would they support my hut?

When I attempted to dig the hole for the fourth post, I ran into trouble. There seemed to be a huge rock hidden underneath the soil. The crowbar didn't go in more than an inch. But if I moved the post the hut wouldn't be square. Maybe I'd have to take the three posts out and start all over again in another place.

In the back of my mind it occurred to me that I might not get any of these posts far enough into the ground to support my hut, but I wasn't quite ready to admit it. And I wouldn't acknowledge something else pushing up from deep inside, suggesting that I might never build this hut at all. I wished I could ask someone for help, but it was supposed to be secret and it was supposed to be *mine*.

Running Barefoot

Sometimes I just sat on the upside-down five-gallon pail and cried.

***

As Mr. Johnson handed back our essays, I was nearly bursting with anticipation. Would he tell the whole class about mine? Would he ask me to read it aloud?

I took my essay from him and eagerly looked for the mark. Sixty percent! I blinked and swallowed. It must be a mistake! My chest tightened uncomfortably. Flipping to the last page, I read the comments in bright red ink: *"Writing skills are excellent, but your idea of a utopia is shallow and unrealistic."*

My eyes burned as I held back tears of humiliation, anger, and defeat.

***

By the end of June I finally had to admit that my garden was not going to grow. I had been anxiously checking the ground for weeks, but only tough weeds and prairie grass had managed to poke through the dense gray soil.

Soon I only went to my clearing every couple of days, then every few days. I didn't take the sledgehammer or the crowbar or the five-gallon pail. I just built a fire and sat for hours, gently tapping the nearest post and staring at it as it teetered back and forth. I didn't cry any more.

One day in August, as I sat in front of my fireplace, I decided I wouldn't go back again. That day, as I walked away from the clearing for the last time, I didn't look back, didn't see the last of the filmy smoke sputtering from the dying fire.

***

Memory is undependable; it invents itself. Maybe it wasn't my essay that made me give up on my hut. Maybe the two events didn't even happen at the same time. But maybe they did; that's how I remember it.

***

My sister and I plough around the circumference of the slough, destroying the smooth perfection of the snow. I can't tell one clearing from the next. The trees have grown, changed, died. I have forgotten. My heart pounds. I'm sweating. Why can't I find it?

Suddenly I trip though a low opening in the bushes and I know that this is it. There's not much here, only untouched snow and three spindly old fence posts leaning against the willows. It really hasn't changed. Yet I'm disappointed, as though I had somehow expected to see my hut standing there, looking as grand as it did in my daydreams of long ago.

I kneel to dig in the snow where I think the fireplace must be. It's not there. I clear away the snow in a huge circle, scratching at the earth and brittle brown grass, but I can't find it. I dig faster. Has it collapsed or is it just buried? Was it ever here? I give up, rise slowly, and stare around me.

My sister breaks the silence, "Let's go! I'm freezing."

I turn away from the clearing to follow her home. "I'd like to come back someday," I say, mostly to myself, "and *really* build it."

The Betrayal of Children

Heather Duff

Someday
we will be loyal
to children
as to old growth firs
wild teddy bears
butterflies
the near-extinct

Some of us
will give children
back to the forest
grant skin to them
roots and heart

They will sprout like fern
pearly everlasting
thyme
rosemary
wild strawberry

They will forgive us

The Boss

Elsie Ellis

I envy you in the tractor cab,
the boss of the farm's operation,
clean and cool in that lofty Case
with air-conditioned comfort.

You have the radio, weather and news,
and jokes from CKRM for a change.
You play a tape: Carroll Baker sings
of the fire of love.

You control the panel, the gauges, the dials.
You watch the combine pick up the swath
from the stubble,
devour, then belch out behind.

"The hopper's full. Come on with the truck,"
the CB crackles. Alert,
I shift the axle into low range
the transmission grinds.

My window up tight
in the stifling heat
keeps out the dirt.
Chaff itches and burns
as sweat wrinkles down my face,
my aching back.

I squint through the dust
churned up by the wheels,
align the truck box just so.
The spout hovers above
to vomit amber durum
until its belly is empty.

You signal, drop back
to fill up the front.
I let up on the gas.
The motor lugs, then stalls.

The grain flows in spirals,
overflows on the cab.
Your hand beckons madly.
Come on!

I read your eyes:
Stupid damn woman!

I quit.
I'm fired.

Suffer curses.
Rehired.

Grit dirt in my teeth.

The Flower of Womanhood

Madeleine Dahlem

Beulah Rose and John had three daughters. They named them Lily, Violet and Pansy. The names had been John's idea; he was the sentimental one. He regretted leaving the civility of Ontario, a well-ordered world where daughters could tat and embroider in velvet-draped parlours—compliant, vulnerable, wilting before noon on a harsh summer's day.

On the prairies, they grew to be big strapping girls, but not quite as handsome as their mother was. Wide-hipped and rangy, they stood loosely, legs wide apart in men's trousers. Their breasts were heavy, filling the workshirts cut from the same cloth as their father's. They learned to work with him and gradually they took over. Lily guided and handled the horses. Pansy rode on the binder, strong limbs working the levers and pedals, her generous buttocks blooming above the molded metal seat. Violet followed behind, gloved hands seizing sheaves and forming them into stooks in one practiced fluid movement.

John was the one who sought the shadows at noon to escape the heat of the day. He fathered a son, whom Beulah Rose named Matthew John Philip. This delicate son of their waning years now bore the hopes and promises of the future. Matthew John Philip was sheltered from the realities of dry land farming, the beating sun and blowing winds, by the labour of his three fond sisters.

On country dance nights, Lily, Violet and Pansy bathed each in turn in the small metal tub set behind the chintz curtain in the first lean-to, the water rationed out from the rain barrel. They washed each other's hair and curled it with heated irons. The smell of singed female hair filled the house, driving the father from it. They slipped printed cotton frocks over their work-hardened bodies and softened their hands with Vaseline.

At the dances, Lily, Violet and Pansy stood first with the women. They placed their cake on the lunch table and listened to talk of babies and death. But they were more comfortable with the men.

Soon, they were outside by the buckboards, hands on hips, talking drought and wheat prices, smoking and nipping from the jug. Although the men admired their strength, their toughness, their wide child-bearing hips, they were intimidated.

But Lily, Violet and Pansy each carried in her heart a secret feminine dream. Lily dreamed of dancing in a creamy satin gown beneath dangling chandeliers. She dreamed of having a touch of consumption, being cared for by a devoted husband. She would rest on a chaise lounge in her parlour and be beautiful in repose.

Violet dreamed of secret lovers whose hands were softer than hers, so soft they could gather flower petals without bruising them. They would speak to her warmly with musical foreign words.

Pansy dreamed of a home, bread baking in the oven, doilies on the furniture, a piano in the front room and a good man to share her day.

When Matthew John Philip turned twenty-one, he came into his own. His father, now old, gave him title to the land. Too delicate to master it, he eventually lost it to the bank and the wind.

When Lily was thirty, walking home from the fields at sundown, she was hit by a freight train. They found scarcely enough of her to fill a shoebox.

Violet never married. She became a cashier at the town's first department store and met lonely men at the luncheonette.

Pansy took a husband who took an ax to her one Sunday afternoon in an alcoholic rage. She survived and lived alone, disfigured. On country-dance nights, she bathed herself and curled her hair with hot irons, the smell of singed female filling the room.

foreclosure

Doris Bircham

it's just dirt,
that's what I thought when I came to this farm
before I saw the field my husband's grandfather
ploughed with a team of oxen, before I walked
inside tipi rings in the east pasture and drank
from a spring bubbling up from the ground before
I watched Canada geese come back and nest year after year
along the creek bank and I heard frogs
in our pasture slough announce spring's arrival
and I planted trees

before I learned to ride with my face to the wind
when I hadn't yet smelled new mown alfalfa or seen heads
heavy with wheat bow beneath the sun

it was before I learned about stillborn calves
or helped feed cattle in a blizzard
and stayed up all night with a heifer
then watched her *mother up* with her newborn calf

when I'd experienced more seed times than harvests
and watched swaths lay for six weeks
rotting in the rain
and after I'd helped trail cattle to their summer pasture
year after year gradually I knew
this is not just dirt, this is our land

all this happened long before our children
picked crocuses on the hillside behind our barn
long before we couldn't find the words to tell them
we have to leave

We Never Looked Back

Lillian Vilborg

We couldn't wait to get out. Regina was too small, too cramped. We knew everybody and couldn't go anywhere without running into someone. So we left on the train at 3:30 in the morning in the dead of winter. We took our two-year-old and whatever we could carry. We didn't look back to see the pain in my mother's eyes or my father's hesitation. We didn't look back as we crossed the windswept prairie, forbiddingly cold, the wind-sculpted snow dancing and posing as we clacked through.

Our bodies welcomed the soft rain, the dingy skies, the twang in the speech of Seattle's friendly people. We were as far west as we could go. In winter it rained and the sky sat on our heads. No blue or gold peeked through for months. Still we did not look back. We explored the forests of dripping pine, the lakes, the rocky shores. People told us how lucky we were to have escaped the plains with their cold, dreary aspect, their emptiness. We glibly agreed.

We never ran into anyone we knew no matter how long we stayed there. We were foreigners with green cards. We couldn't vote. It was exotic. We were exotic. And happy. We explored the mountains. We didn't pine.

Sometimes we returned to our country for a visit. Fifteen hundred miles from Regina we ran into people we knew. "Canada is really a small town," we commented.

The rhododendrons bloomed in spring—showy, extravagant, deep pinks and reds. "The rhodies are out," we said. Then came the hydrangeas: huge sensuous blooms in shades of blue. Climbing roses covered the garage, all preceded by the forsythia's profusion of yellow on bare branches. We had never seen anything like it.

Blue sky came and our spirits soared. Our discoveries piled one on top of the other as we camped at minus tide, picked clams and mussels, caught fish from ocean-going boats, admired huge trees, were amazed at rocks, praised the mountains—the Cascades, the Olympics, and most majestic, Mount Rainier. "The mountains are out," we said when we saw them ringing our city.

We took the train home in the summer to visit, go to the lake, erase the pain from my mother's eyes. It was the same hot, windy, dry, bleak place: the southern prairie. I didn't miss it. Not at all.

I didn't know why I was crying as the train pulled out in the dusk of dawn, headed back to our exotic new land. My eyes scanned the horizon that blossomed into light. Nothing blocked the vista of golden wheat and barley and oats as far as I could see in every direction. Grain gradually gave way to rolling, light brown hills with bands of antelope roaming alongside the train as it clacked its way back to soft rain, low clouds, exotic flowers.

We never looked back. We were never lonely. We were on our own and life was exciting. Seattle was one of the most beautiful places in the world. We would never see everything we wanted to see. Then, visiting the mighty Pacific as it rolled in whitecapped, we said, "It looks like the Saskatchewan prairie in winter. It looks like the moonlight bouncing off the swirling snow."

In spring we didn't look for crocuses peeking through snow because there weren't any. We didn't raise our noses to the fragrance of lilacs. We didn't wonder whether the caragana's yellow had bloomed, if the soft pink of the prairie rose was dotting all the roadside ditches. We were happy with the profusion that is the West Coast. We weren't lonely.

But from some deep place in ourselves that had no words we realized that we wanted to go home: to feel the aliveness of the biting wind, the challenge of the fierce cold, the warmth of the brilliant sun, the stretch of blue sky, the immensity of the prairie landscape.

We just wanted to go home.

Sunday Drive

Lorie Miseck

I wish the bonnetless, gloveless
Sunday afternoons back.
The blue ship of a car with sharp fins,
roads loose with gravel and dust.
Tail lights round and red
with intention, bright as devil's eyes.

In the back, pinched between sisters,
chin in hand, elbows on knees, feet
on the black hump of the car's spine.
My mother's hand on my father's thigh,
her clear blue scarf, a bandage of rollers, his hand

on the steering wheel, the other shifting
gears from first, to second, to third,
punching the radio's black buttons
as if today the sound will be different, clearer –
each hit returning a hiss or a faded voice
from a city we've never seen.

What would I tell them if I were back
in this room of wheels?

Drive a little slower?
Pull over near the raspberry bush,
eat more than you save,
let the juice slide down our throats?
Eat them well and slowly,
the future has lost its taste buds.

Or would I just say
remember this.

Tell them to breathe in deeply
the smell of dust and vinyl,
ham sandwiches wrapped in wax paper,
juice in jam jars.

Would I say that sometimes
there is nothing more than this:
smell and taste?

Would I say let the dog running
along the ditch catch us today?
Stop, give him water,
let him jump in the back
and nuzzle at our feet.

Would I tell them the worries that
fidget their minds are useless?
The new job will work out,
there will be food and money –
enough to get by.

Would I say you'll be thrown
so far from this place,
even the map will be lost?
There will be a cut so deep
years will fall in the wound.
There will be survivors.
And not.

Or would I say
drive, drive to where the sun ends,
drive to that place where our breath is one,
drive into the shade of dark
where our faces are so known to each other,
they are familiar even in shadow.
Then let us take the long way home.

Grave of the Saw-Whet

Heather Duff

Wind whipping through shreds of his Canadian flag on deck. The maple leaf and its two pink stripes faded into white. It looks like a flag of surrender, which, in a sense, it is. I look out at the grey water of Sechelt Inlet, at rust-coloured rocks, a dead jellyfish glued to the beach, a fleet of overturned motor boats paint scratched by barnacles and splintered canoes. The herring skiff floats in balance, in tandem with the raft.

"Why don't you want to have children?" I ask him. My heart cramps, a ghost uterus. It's not really children I want. It's the idea of children. The idea is metaphysical oxygen.

"With what's happening on the planet, I think it's terribly cruel to have children," he says. "Look what a mess we're leaving them. They'll hate us for not doing more. I guess it's our guilt we can't deal with."

So, now childless is a bloody moral imperative.

I'm going to die. At least death is one rite of passage I won't miss out on. This is consolation of sorts, although it does not stop the tears that burst from the catacomb of my belly.

"You know you're my last chance man, on account of my age."

"Yeah, I know."

"Is this the official decision, then?"

"Yes."

"What if you're on your death bed someday, and you look back and regret this decision? What if there are no descendents to visit you and everyone you know, your peers, have already died?"

"I'll never be on my death bed. One day, I'll just walk out into that salal there."

Silence for two minutes, or thirty. Grant watches my face distort for awhile as if it is a landscape, then looks out at a splintered plank floating on the water.

"Last week, I buried a saw-whet owl up on the bluff," he says. "Tiny, 'bout six inches long, with grey spots. Found her drowned in a cookie batter bucket I had used to bail out the old tank up there. You know that cookie batter you can buy pre-made? Saw-whets live in old growth, eh, like the old growth up behind the bluff, and here this one human intrusion, a damned cookie batter bucket, and a few inches of rain water. And hell, that was it."

Do you like the name Shelagh for a girl?

At the end of August, Grant and I sit in the canoe eating hazelnuts from a plastic bag, by the small salt-water marsh with a view of the cave that heralds pictographs from 700 AD. I stare at the vast rock face that guards them. "Now I know why the artist chose that spot," I say. "There's a bear in that rock."

"No way," says Grant. "Where?"

I point to the rock bluff. "See the giant eyes, nose, upper back? Unmistakably a bear."

"Of course. I see it now," he says. "It must've been a sacred place."

"Miraculous." I mutter. "We both see the same thing."

"Finally, eh?"

"Bear Rock."

Silence but for the swish of paddles in the sea. "I'm sorry about the baby thing," says Grant.

"I know."

"Several women from my lurid past were pregnant but decided they didn't want me or the babies. The worst was the last. Ruthie. She called me up one night, said: 'By the way I aborted twins today. Yours.' "

Tears drip on to my life jacket but he doesn't see because I'm in the bow.

"I could, at least, still fight for the forest."

"Let's see how close we can get before it stops looking like a bear."

We paddle towards Bear Rock, then stop in front of it, watching the shades of grey, green, black.

We reach the shore and tie up the canoe to a stump and start to climb Bear Rock, which pulls us irresistibly towards the top. On the left side of the rock, there's a cleft of earth, salal, and a few arbutus trees with peeling red bark. Someone has tied a long rope there to a fir at the top of the bluff. Grant tests it to make sure it will hold our weight. Slowly, we pull ourselves by the rope through a sea of salal, wind blown, waves of it, tough and well-rooted; it scratches our bare legs.

Grant reaches a ledge at the top and helps me up on to it, reaches long fingers toward me, like a Michelangelo painting. I clasp his fingers. It is often our fingers intersecting when words cannot, or a shred, stone, pad of earth, delicate pattern on tree bark, lone honk of goose, high nest of osprey. Now, mossy hillsides up on top behind Bear Rock, with a spectacular view of the peak of Mount Richardson through fir, hemlock, alder. We lie down in the moss. Grant wraps his arms around me. I don't know where the moss ends and Grant begins. I am deep in a nest of my own choosing. We don't make love. There is no need to, but just to lie there, breathing like feathers, the opening and closing of lichen flower, tickle of wild chives on thigh. Tears dried by the wind that comes down from the mountain, dry tight riverbeds from eye to chin.

"Alright," says Grant.

It's three in the morning. The moon is full and lights up the whole inlet like a bright lamp. Clouds everywhere, backlit, the down in a donkey's ear. It's time to turn. The bright side of the moon, the bright side of bright. My ovaries glow like the moons of Jupiter.

Labour Day. I ovulate here in the moving forest, like a doe, silent, brave, into dry and brittle cedars from the long scorch of summer. Afraid the past will snatch it all away. I lie and wait for my lover amid the trees. He finally comes, moving up through the salal bush, his eyes furtive like those of a marten. He lies down on still waters; I receive him into my belly. I conceive in the forest by the grave of the saw-whet owl, marked by a cairn of stones. My child of the forest is crying already; what forest is left is like the brittle frames of old women standing. If this spark caught in one of those dry firs, it would spread like wildfire. It is the one hope of the earth, to conceive amid lost trees, some blackened old growth trunks from a fire sixty years ago. And new growth—fir, cedar, hemlock, a few maples. To conceive in the wilderness, that something can still grow.

The next day, Grant and I canoe to a stone we call the Chesterfield that overlooks the entrance to Salmon Inlet, Kunechin. There is the skeleton of a fawn washed up in the eddies of rocks, parts of a skull, thighbones, vertebrae. Black crabs crawl through the eye sockets. "Must've tried to swim," says the father of the forest child, "But got swept away in the current."

The forest child in my belly grows. I feel dizzy, flush, nauseated for days. I must keep her alive; this is my calling. She is myself, or not. I do not know for sure. When I feel sick I talk to her, feel her moving.

There is no proof except for this black spark, waiting. It could be my own sacrifice. In the black spark there is a pinprick light, like a miner's headlamp six miles down to hell.

"I want *this* baby," I tell Grant. "Not a baby later when we're sure we're ready, but this baby."

I take folic acid, have warm baths that aren't too hot. Avoid jumps in my dance class, wine and everything else with the label, contraindicated. I do everything right and when, back in the bush the blood pours down my leg I believe I am still pregnant and I don't take anything to relieve the pain. I lie curled in a cave of pillows and whimper at this nameless night. This blood keeps pouring from my body, blood with no home.

If only I could name this blood that turns noon into night.

The blood is not Shelagh.

I squat over a plastic bucket until it is full of my dead spark, indistinguishable, like heavy menstrual period, nothing more. I put on my rubber boots, grab the garden trowel and climb the hill lined with salal. I hike up past the chopped cedar, with its rings cut for shakes to cover the roof of the new wood shed. I walk past the old growth fir, leaning slightly toward the earth, blackened on one side by that fire in the 1930's. I climb up to the high perch overlooking the river otter's den, the bay, the inlet with its glinting water. I find the rocks that mark the spot, by some wild garlic and tiger lily.

It is the end of my childbearing years.

This is the gravesite, where my lover put a dead owl into the earth one night. I dig a rocky hole beside the rocks and into it I pour the bucket of blood. I bury my womb, or is it my living heart, in a shallow grave by the saw-whet owl. I sob and look out at the dark water. The sea aches to speak.

The saw-whet owl calls the name of my forest child, calls, calls until she can resist no longer. Her blood rises up from the earth and high into a sky that breathes no words. My dead child is somewhere in the cracked earth, and up in the sky full of seaplanes and a refurbished American bomber streaking fuel through this Canadian sky. She rises up and bleats with wild mountain lambs, swims with otters, fishes with loons. Her voice is the voice of all girls and women, both birthing and dying, both the sistered and the sisterless.

Animal scent trails me to these two obscure graves that have nothing and everything in common.

IV
Seeing in the Dark

We who are born of a star
Who then are we?

Born of A Star
Carolyn McDade

Born of a Star

© 1998 by Carolyn McDade

   Running Barefoot

Born of A Star

Carolyn McDade

Return
Return to the darkness, return
this longest night of wonder
Return
Return to the dream return
this holy night to ponder
Deep in the night, listen
listen
Turn to the light
waken, waken
Deep in the night turn to the light
Waken to Sun's ancient summons -
We who are born of a star
who then are we?
we who are loved by a star
who then love we?

We who are born of a star
who then are we?

Arctic

Catherine MacLean

Dark embraces all this land
      land protected from rash wind
      by dull layer of ice
      home of white bear and ragged ptarmigan

Dark hurled through wildcolour
      unfurled around, to catch me up in ecstasy
      refraction of storms on
      long-forgotten face of sun

Dark embraces me on this land,
      arms warm with intimacy,
      lips sealing mine from unimportant talk
      thrills me 'round with colour:
            indigo of passion
            green of hope
            red of lifeblood

This dark, I know,
      will let me go
      will bring me to the quiet light of spring
      the shameless bright of summer

But I bid it stay –
      this land too large under sunlight
            too wide to comprehend
            too big for me
      I prefer the sensual dance of colour,
      the braiding,
free in dark's huge mirror of solar flame;
      the bold yellow dawn draws too clearly.

The shadow of dark I understand;
this much I can know.

Click Beetle

Valerie Stetson

I have to live in every country
of my province
and learn new vocabularies
of dreams and weather
overlook the cherries
a migrant picker overlooks
my voice hidden by
blue lamp lit shadow
my tent, seen from the road
orange with firelight

make sloe gin on my potato
co-op with the woman who
cut up her wedding dress
to make lampshades
the wind smelling of my earth

become the caver whose body is
rubbed all over by unworldly walls
squashing my chocolate bar
in pedigreed night
remove my head lamp
to swim in rock-covered tunnels
guessing when to emerge

bathe in outdoor tubs overlooking
clear-cut valleys
and imagine them treed

right myself like a click beetle
in a chamber pot province
its menus, accent, generosity,
pick-up lines and wintering birds
estranging me

Learning the Land

Eunice Victoria Scarfe

We could go by boat, I said in November of 1970, sitting on the floor
of our cold Yorkshire flat. My husband had just accepted a position at
the University of Alberta and we were searching for the city of
Edmonton in his Philips' school atlas. Canada was given one page; the
counties of England were given ten pages. Canada looked small on its
page. We had to squint to read the names in small print: Cypress Hills,
Drumheller, Dunvegan, Peace River, Saskatchewan, Medicine Hat, and a
city called Edmonton, slung on the same latitude as the city of Leeds
where we sat. Edmonton, Alberta, the most northern Canadian city of
significant population, though not the most northern city. Edmonton,
Alberta, with its back to the mountains and its face to the prairie.

We landed in Edmonton on a clear January night in 1971 with a
temperature of minus 40. We didn't need to ask whether it was
Celsius or Fahrenheit.

The cab driver drove us north down Calgary Trail to Saskatchewan
Drive and stopped not far from the Strathcona apartment where we
were to stay. He wanted us to see the view of the river and the
Edmonton skyline.

We thanked him for the tour, not expecting that our entire life in
Edmonton would be spent in sight of that skyline. A home in Mill
Creek built in 1912 on land deeded to *Jenny Skinner, Widow.* A
professional life at the University of Alberta. Friends in Skunk Hollow,
Old Strathcona and Garneau. Children's birthday parties celebrated at
Queen Elizabeth Park. Swimming at Kinsmen Pool. Fireworks watched
from the top of Scona Hill. Cycling in the river valley communities of
Cloverdale and Riverdale and Rossdale. The names run together were,
and still are, like music to me.

We hadn't expected a river zipping two halves of a city together. We
hadn't expected land as flat as the sea. Hadn't the map shown
mountains nearby? We hadn't expected a thriving theatre and opera
and symphony and university. We hadn't expected such an
extravagant bowl of blue and bright sky.

Both of us had visited Canada once. We were ignorant of this land
and its people. He had been to Montreal for the Expo in 1967. I had

once sailed to Victoria on the Princess from Seattle. He knew that Canadians spoke French. I knew that Canadians served afternoon tea. We knew nothing of Alberta. We didn't know that Head-Smashed-In Buffalo Jump was older than the Egyptian pyramids, that the markings at Writing-On-Stone made up the largest body of native petrographs on the North American continent, that the highway between Montana and Calgary followed the oldest Indian trail in the Americas. We didn't know the colour of canola or the devastation of the Frank slide, the location of Leduc oil or that homesteading was still possible in the Peace River Country. We hadn't yet seen sun dogs or prairie dogs or heard that there were no rats in Alberta. We hadn't awakened to a chinook or rushed outside to embrace the sight of northern lights or view the slow symphony of a midsummer sunset.

And we didn't know that Alberta in 1971 was less than 75 years old.

We made a map to the scale of our life and in making the map, we invented our life. For absent relatives, we substituted families who like us had no living—or dead—relatives in this country of Canada, families who, also far away from Alberta, had poured over inadequate maps which had concealed as much as they revealed of this place Alberta, maps that had never revealed the land of Alberta or the lives of Albertans.

We were immigrants, though not always seen as such, either by others or by ourselves. *Immigrant*, we discovered, implied arriving empty-handed, speaking a language other than English, fleeing from persecution or distress. We hadn't come empty-handed. We spoke English. We hadn't fled. We were, however, experiencing the ambiguity, ignorance and anxiety of relocation. If immigrant also meant a person who comes to a country to take up permanent residence, we were immigrants.

The first morning in Edmonton we walked from 100th Street, where our apartment faced King Edward School, to Whyte Avenue and then on to the University. Our walk that day defined a postage stamp of Canada we travelled hundreds of times in the eighteen years: west from Mill Creek to the University, east from the University to the Creek.

The skyline we saw across the Saskatchewan River so many years ago became familiar and known and ours, a *cloud of witnesses* watching our life here on the south side of the North Saskatchewan River, a

mural of storefronts not unlike the false and true storefronts of
Sinclair Ross' town of Horizon in his seminal text *As For Me and My
House.*

Alberta is not a hinterland, and never was, though some have said as
much. Alberta is where you live near land and in land, where you can't
escape land, and where summer and winter, sunrise and sunset, you
are held by land. A plain landscape, a landplace. Theodore Roethke
could have been speaking of this place when he wrote:

> *I learned not to fear Infinity,*
> *The far field, the windy cliffs of forever.*

> *What we love is near, at hand,*
> *Always, in earth and air.*[1]

What we learned was the land, this land that is now home.

---

[1] Theodore Roethke. "The Far Field," from the collection of the same name. NY:
Doubleday, 1964, p.27.

Love Affair

Jean Fahlman

It is a love/hate smoldering affair
which possesses me in vice-like embrace.
I have tried sometimes to leave her,
when she is frigid and unyielding,
when she seems to taunt my devotion.

I stay, though I grow weary
of this intense spiritual tie.
She is so needy . . . so demanding.
Still, I drink in her fragrance,
the mother-earth scent of her fertility
her charm, her baffling capricious ways.

When we are apart I long for the solid feel of her
solid, even though I know her for a drifter,
forever shifting with the prairie winds.
Her changing image has seared my flesh,
her mark is branded upon my soul.

She lives within my heart, her blood
throbs dark and rich in my veins,
this ageless seducer who owns me.
I can never leave her, never give up
the land.

Coyote

Therese Noonan

Through pale eyes Winter watches her
struggle three-legged
across a well gnawed ridge
of frost heaved rock scattered bone
a cold wind taunts her
with scent days old
its icy laughter lashes ahead
then cuts back
to count coup on her rime-manged ribs

done for bellied low
she hears the frightened howlings
trapped in the ravening wind
pups born too late
souls taken to ghost the darkness
lift small voices up
in the ancient song of dying
hungers added to the wild call
of a mother to the goddess Moon

pale-eyed Winter stalks her
forgets that she's the hunter
over the bodies of her children
she waits yellow eyes gleaming
sinks broken fangs deep
into the famine of her own bones
sucks Winter's shattered marrow
silver blood melting snow

Trickster Changer the She-Coyote
circles back counts coup
on the wind loping three-legged
the trail taken by Spring

Whiteout

Vivian Hansen

Marianne could easily see unusual things after a long night of marking papers. This was her third late night; the clock on her car panel glowed 1:30. As she drove home from the university, prairie wind blew wraith-like snow fingers into the road in front of her. Marianne was wary. She could not outrace the fingers, had to move with them, allow them to guide her along. If she were to let the car go where the snow fingers pulled she would end up with the other abandoned cars already lining the base of Nose Hill. The drivers of those cars had made the mistake of trying to outdrive the whiteout conditions. Marianne tried to crawl her car along the snow wall to her den in the lee of the hill.

She reviewed tomorrow's notes in her mind. The first year poetry students were struggling with the material, and she was attempting a few creative ways to introduce the concept of beat, metrics, scansion. Once she had even tried waltzing around the classroom to some three-quarter-time poetry beat. But that movement was the past, in a place when her skin and blood shivered with the ecstasy of life.

Now things were different. Blacker than Winter Solstice. A wave of fatigue crawled over her. The effort to remain alert was almost too much, but she managed to find her way. Nose Hill was obscured in Solstice Night. Marianne parked the car and switched off the engine, achingly eager to drop into bed. An almost imperceptible movement in the periphery of her vision made her look around. A neighbor's dog stood in the middle of the street, her stance odd and somehow unfamiliar. Marianne was about to call the dog but stopped, decided to watch instead.

It was not a dog but a lone wolf—a silver bitch, her stance proud and curious, staring back at Marianne. They were alone with each other in the hushed stillness. Solitary and fey, woman-eyes and wild dog-eyes locked, a moment of merge.

Marianne blinked first. She could not tell when she opened her eyes if the wolf had slipped away into the night, or if she herself had fallen asleep curled into the driver's seat. All she knew was a terrible cold seeping through her fur coat, and she was still not in bed. She would not get warm before morning.

Vignettes of her life—recollections surfacing in the cold. The doctor's voice loud, sudden, like the blast of a radio in the callous cold of a car.

"It's named for the sign of the crab. Cancer. Legs and claws seem to spread out from its body, and like the crab, cancer can spread out too. It naturally invades normal tissues and organs so before it does that, we must attempt to destroy the diseased cells."

The doctor's commentary had reminded Marianne of her own strategy of teaching poetry students, only the doctor made no move to dance. Instead, he found something else that worked for him, a way to tell someone that they had Cancer. They. Not Marianne. Shock stung her body like electrical currents. She tried to control the stings by concentrating on the metaphor: the crab. Becoming something Other. Transformative. She could almost picture the crab tentacles stir from the site of her diseased breast, migrating—to where? All she could do was feel the lump, probably growing even as she examined its hardness. Words eluded her. She who had always known what to do with them.

She dutifully tried the chemotherapy, followed the prescribed routine of healing; a different kind of shamanism, one with white coats and opaque skipping ropes seeking her blood. Nothing gave her peace. Her mind resisted the physical connections, gesturing ever deeper to the understandings of her own heart. Vignettes of re-membering.

***

The vignette grew warmer; classroom and a soft caress of poetry.

"So what sort of effect does Marvell achieve in his use of subjunctive verb tense in *To His Coy Mistress?*"

Blank stares. Marianne waited. Sometimes it helped to wait a suitable few minutes to see if a thinking student might figure it out. No one did.

"Subjunctive verb tense. *Had we but world enough, and time/ This coyness, lady, were no crime.* The subjunctive verb mood launches the notion of potentials and possibilities. We are called to imagine . . . For instance, Marvell used the subjunctive as a form of persuasion, possibly to pursue his lady."

She lectured on about imagining, all the while gripping the reality of this moment. This moment in the lecture hall when she still had both her breasts, and her life.

> But at my back I always hear
> Time's winged chariot hurrying near;
> And yonder all before us lie
> Deserts of vast eternity.[1]

The lump in her breast crawled up to her throat, and a horrible fear threatened to strangle her. She stood staring out at this crowd of students. She'd never felt uncomfortable with them before now.

"Dr. Wells?" began one of them. Marianne started, clutching her throat to arrest the claw of the crab that crawled up to her tongue. Was she really standing there, allowing this white air to engulf them all? She clutched at the thought, which floated comfortingly like a log in the water.

"People, it's clear that we'll get no further with Marvell today. Let's shut this down early. I want you to be thinking about the subjunctive verb tense. To imagine . . . " She wasn't sure that any of them heard her above the scuffling and closure of desks.

***

Was the she-wolf an apparition? Was there really a wolf here in the lee of Nose Hill, where only coyotes prowled? Was the dog-creature really a coyote? Where had it come from? Wolves were wood creatures, and there were no woods around here. There were a few poplar groves on Nose Hill where coyotes might hang out, but that was it.

Marianne rather liked thinking about the mysterious wolf, enjoying the distraction from real life, papers, lectures, the monotony of the university. She wanted the bitch to be more than an apparition.

She was preparing the next day's lecture selections half-heartedly, could smell the reek of her own unwashed body. Her remaining breast hung listlessly. She slid her fingers through thinning raven hair

---

[1] All quotes from: Marvell, Andrew. "To His Coy Mistress". **Norton Anthology of Poetry**, third edition. W.W. Norton & Co. New York, 1983.

speckled with grey. She glanced at her toes; small and dainty, touching earth like divining tools. They had fallen into disuse, and she resolved to correct that. She put the book down on the coffee table in front of her. She was just reading words without comprehension. She closed her eyes, resting the back of her head against the chair, checking her eyelids for cracks. Thinking about David, with whom she had shared books, wine, and the taste of each other's bodies. Sounding him.

"David, I need my copies of *Lord of the Rings.*"

"Haven't got them, Marianne."

"You have. Must have. I can't find them anywhere." She heard the depth of his lovely voice, negotiating, penetrating her memory and the dark, callous cold of her house. Instead of returning her old copies, David had presented her with a leather-bound set for Christmas.

She couldn't really find fault with David anymore. She was too tired, and all the little irritations blew off her like rotting crabapples in spring. The marriage was over. There remained only the books, and the pleasant sense of being allowed to imagine anything.

Who could she talk to about the Cancer, the Big C? Surely not David. Even while they were married, she realized the impossibility of talking to him about anything save the most mundane matters. Her Cancer, her breast, discussing the disease that now infected the soft folds of flesh that had once given him pleasure—this he wouldn't do. He would think the conversation contagious, as though he had tasted—ingested—her disease.

A sleep of sorts. Her sleep heavier now with the innate need of her body to heal itself, to chop off the arms of the crab and wither its tentacles. Marvelous ability to heal. Marvell.

> *Thy Beauty shall no more be found;*
> *Nor, in thy marble Vault, shall sound*
> *My echoing Song: the Worms shall try*
> *That long preserv'd Virginity . . .*

The music of the poetry passed her into a deep slumber.

Once upon a time her bed had to be made comfortable, nest-like, before she could sleep. That had all changed with the coming of the Crab. She was now able to sleep anywhere, imagining the macrophages attacking the tumor. She talked to the tumor, although the surgeons had assured her that all the cancerous cells were hacked off. She remembered a nurse friend saying that in first-year anatomy, the instructors were all too willing to hack a breast from a cadaver. It was just fatty flesh, after all, easily removed from the body. Marianne had taken comfort in the callous knowing of that practice. Even so, she had the sense that some of her enemy still remained and she would have to call a truce or come to a confrontation while she still possessed enough strength to negotiate.

For weeks, she searched for Wolf outside her living room window. "Where are you, Wolf? What can I say to conjure you back to this house?" Wolf did not respond. Nor did Marianne expect that she would. It was just nice to test her voice at something—anything. She didn't expect to see Wolf by day, of course, but late at night with her house lights turned down, she searched, praying that the vision would be real and not just a deception of sleep. The looking, searching, continued for several weeks. There were papers to be corrected, exams to be marked and all the while, the day visits of chemotherapy that made her horridly ill.

She felt the sand shift in her brain; a small hourglass in her head signaled the passage of time and a shift of reality. She kept checking the sand, turning it mentally upside down for the fear that she expected to find and confront. The fear that she couldn't seem to locate.

Wolf might know where the fear was, and how to attack.

The shifting sand might be hormonal, or a reaction to chemotherapy. Either way, Marianne decided to pay attention to the feeling. Perhaps it was a warning of some kind, an indicator that her body needed some other element in order to heal. Just what that "other" really was, she had no idea. Sooner or later, it would slip out of the sand and over her fingers like the purity of a pearl emerging from the slime of an oyster. She felt sure of it.

Marianne reasoned that perhaps Wolf was to be found on Nose Hill. She hardly knew where to look, but when winter yielded to spring, she realized she wouldn't freeze when the wind blew off the distant glaciers, sweeping the hill clean of people. Tiny tips of crocuses thrust out of the ground, tufting the hill with a mauve blush, softening harsh winter grasses. She didn't hear any voice except the wind, moaning cold breath against the remains of her body. She ceased to test her own voice except to sing wordlessly and listen to sounds that the wind made, caressing the hill. Her hikes yielded often to coulees, where snow lay abandoned like white quilts over grass. She perceived more of the miniscule life around her, noticing the mouse burrows that tunneled furtively from beneath the snow-quilts. Once she stayed until dusk when the animals emerged. Her thermos of coffee kept her warm until then. She felt sure she would spot the Wolf-Bitch soon.

***

Marianne became aware of the skrtch-skrtch of movement. She had nestled next to mouse tunnels, her scarf, hat, and fur coat cutting the wind. The sand in her brain shifted, and she no longer thought of herself as human or distinct from the space around her. The Crab gnawed at her breast like a skrtch-skrtch of knowing, hearing the mouse but not seeing it. One did not need to see: just imagine. Imagining was as real as the air around her. If she did not move, she would see.

Wolf emerged from behind a willow, white, her silver flecks glinting in the glowing caress of a high full moon. She was stealthy, lifting one paw delicately over a mound of old snow, amber eyes studying Marianne inquisitively.

Marianne was still, prostration necessary to the meeting of minds. Wolf sniffed, catching a sense of illness, disease, the sweat of abjection. Stealing closer, she examined Marianne's face, eyes, then slid a long pink tongue over exposed flesh. Wolf tongued all the crags of Marianne's face—coulees of ears, erratic of nose, nuzzling eyes, soft lips of mouthflesh—caressing the balance of life. Marianne forgot her own name, but knew that even if the Crab lingered in her breast, Wolf had healed her soul.

***

"I'm ever so sorry, Marianne," mumbled the oncologist, "But it seems that we have been unable to arrest the Cancer."

Marianne heard the carefully structured sentence and the unveiled pain in her doctor's prognosis. She felt the strength to feel sorry for him, but not for herself. Wolf had changed all that. Since the Night of the Wolf's Tongue, as she now called it, her face and body tingled with the warmth of life. If her personal Crab refused to yield to that knowing, too bad.

"Depending on the tenacity of the tumor," the doctor struggled on, "you need to give yourself three to six months."

She smiled at him serenely, anxious to be rid of his burden. "Thank you, doctor. I will take care of myself."

He was perplexed, she could see that. Wondering if she had lost her mind. Yes, thankfully, she had. He left then, closing the door softly behind him, leaving her to her place, the landscape of her soul.

Somewhere in the zephyr of time remaining to her, Marianne shed the skin of humanity. She made her will, leaving the house and all its contents, including *Lord of the Rings*, to David. She deliberately neglected the flowerbeds, the lawn, and refused to disturb the dust on the furniture. Instead, she roamed the Hill, finding her final space, and waiting for Wolf, who found her at night.

As summer progressed and the Crab advanced, Wolf licked Marianne's remaining breast every day, easing the cancerous lumps. She toked on marijuana to ease pain, and found herself still able to walk. During the day, Marianne sought the soft mauve tops of bergamot that begged to be picked. At night, she slept naked in the coulees, bringing only a sleeping bag for warmth. Sometimes she trekked downhill to her house and went about her human business, shape-shifting as necessity demanded, returning whatever phone calls she still felt compelled to respect. She was free to read and spend time with Wolf. This much of the life she had remaining to her she coveted for herself, and besides, how would she ever explain her absence to Wolf?

The fall would be theirs.

When the leaves on the Hill turned into their burnished copper, Marianne bought winter outdoor sleeping equipment, a heavier sleeping bag, and a small stove to brew the bergamot she had dried from the summer's yield. She ate very little. Crackers. Cheese. Scotch, straight. She bought a roll of sausage and shared it with Wolf. By now, Wolf nuzzled her closely, as though anticipating the end.

Marianne welcomed the cold now, as the fall chilled into November and the first snow arrived, fluffy over her tent mound. She had refused further chemotherapy, asked her doctor to save the radiation for someone who might still be able to use it. Something lingered of Marvell: "Thus, though we cannot make our sun/Stand still, yet we will make him run." It was a chant, one that she saved from her human days; the incantatory words still had a purpose for her. Otherwise, she had no further use for human communication, only nuzzling Wolf and whining softly, sometimes moaning in the primal passions of life and death.

She allowed her thoughts to drift peacefully into the black of a Nose Hill night, stars sprinkling dust into her eyes as she slept nestled in the Wolf's fur.

In icy dark, the Winter Solstice blanketed Nose Hill. It was about that time that a White Wolf emerged from the black of a coulee where She had lived and kept vigil for some months. She was accompanied by an even larger Silver Wolf, who ran with the snow-fingers that beckoned unknowing drivers into the winter storms of Nose Hill.

Requiem
For Caren Forest

Heather Duff

Road entitled *Danger: Active Falling*
hurls dust up from rubber treads
I consider locking myself
to this parked truck
amid eyes of coyote
lean torches in the trees.

With rare spirits
I carve shapes in the air
over rusted cables
through shards of granite
as tails like forbidden rudders
sail shadows of coyote
through waves of salal in mourning

Until dawn
on a stage with no escape
we spirits dance
to clank of leghold traps
and the family men light butts
dock their whitewashed boat
black boxes crammed
with pastrami on kaisers
they watch us from behind caffeine eyes
whet saws that will fund their childrens' university

I listen to the pant of coyote
and to the thicket, a sobbing heart
my own or the quiet heart of history

It is the end of something older than
1800 year old yellow cedar

It could be the death
of death

Buckhorn Mountains

Linda Wikene Johnson

I planted the burned space
walked in the underbrush
smelled the fireweed
assessed the growth
of small cactus spruce
and lank young firs
I walked the copper hills
where the moose jolt their run
saw the green-gold hesitant stream
wind into the northland
I estimated the browse and blight
tied government silver tags on trees
like licenses on wolves
my hands bled from the needles
my cheeks stung in the Indian summer wind
all in wilderness
fireweed
the afterburn
the sparse
dazed
staggered
green
after
flame

Holy Ground

Marianne Worcester

I was born within sight of the mountains and a long stone's throw from English Bay, washed in with the Fraser River flood of 1948. By the time I was aware that my life was taking place in any particular landscape, however, I was living far inland on the coast of a more ancient sea. Every other year we drove back across the prairies to British Columbia to visit family. Like pilgrims making our way from one holy site to another, we would touch down briefly in Banff, Jasper, Lake Louise, Rogers Pass, breathless with wonder and awe, expecting the miraculous. I anticipated these exposures to spectacular vistas as much as I yearned for the last day of school, Santa Claus or a Marilyn Munroe figure.

During that Winnipeg adolescence I kept a scrapbook which I called my B.C. Book. In it I pasted calendar cut outs of mountains, seascapes, dark forests, stupendous waterfalls. In the long periods between the trips to paradise, I collected images of that *true home*, creating a kind of sacred text to which I offered secret devotion. Had I been a Catholic I would perhaps have been able to explain this activity to myself. The pictures of the desired landscape were like prayer beads, a rosary of inchoate longing for something they represented—something exotic and wild, like angels or Incarnation.

I knew this to be a dubious preoccupation for a girl in a Protestant evangelical faith community. Our belief system abhorred external aids to devotion and was suspicious of such expressions of passion for the natural world that might detract the created from the Creator. Although I faithfully and even passionately searched the Bible for the divine revelation hidden there, I did not abandon the sacred texts of the earth itself or the intuitive knowledge I carried of my connection to the *things* of this world. I was always in danger of being misunderstood.

I had a curious predilection for poetry and *mooning*, particularly when more mundane tasks beckoned, and so I learned to be careful, to keep my inexplicable loves hidden. The scrapbook grew thicker as I added poems by Pauline Johnson, my high priestess of landscape and longing. Then came Wordsworth, Coleridge and Keats, the English romantics in our school texts, who seemed to share my longing for a kind of intimacy with nature, dignifying it with weighty philosophies which some adults thought worthy of discussion, even truthful. In this way my feelings for nature became more formalized, even possible to articulate.

The eroticized landscapes of the English Lake District or Italy did not exactly map on to the banks of the Red and Assiniboine Rivers, and Windermere was certainly not Winnipeg. And yet the connection between beauty and spirit in landscape itself had been made. This connection lay in a reality outside of metaphor or analogy. I knew that the natural world did not just point to something else, it was complete in itself, and I was part of it, like stars and grass. I learned the term *pantheist* and applied it to myself like a small stigmata, marvelling in secret.

Why do some landscapes resonate to a frequency within the minded body while others simply remain pleasant places we have visited or lived in? It was the vast, tumultuous coastal landscapes which called to my imagination, my temperament somehow ill-suited to flat prairie expanses with their unbroken skylines, broad earth-bearing rivers, the endless months of bone breaking cold. I yearned for younger, craggier mountains, unattainable snowy peaks, plunging waters, bottomless gorges, Odyssean seas, and moisture that didn't freeze but bred an effulgence of green upon green.

And suddenly, in my early twenties, I was there, catapulted into my imaginal home by a precipitous marriage. Within days came the first of many tests of the depth of my commitment to my partner and to this Eden-like place. The first test had to do with boats. I had unwittingly married a man who expected me to go with him out onto the sea and up into the mountains, not just to look at them but to go there. I had not grown up with wilderness experience. I had to learn to trust his experience and my own instincts, to explore and survive in this new home if this is where I intended to remain.

Each excursion away from home was an act of faith, a free fall into the unknown, preceded by a night-long convulsion of fear. It wasn't a lesson I could learn after the second or third try or even in a year or two. With every venture the cycle of refusal, fear, resignation, relinquishment, and then, occasionally joy, had to be gone through. This beloved picture book landscape was not only fantastically real, it was also unpredictable and treacherous. Poems became pleas for safe crossings; each portal a jumping off place where burnt offerings seemed more in order than photographs. Fear and desire, and what I now think of as a Loving Unseen Hand, propelled me into this new country of marriage and landscape.

Eventually exploration led to cultivation and with the arrival of babies a need for stability, safety and more predictability. During this time we made several forays to Gambier Island, a large fist between Bowen Island and the Sunshine Coast. It is mostly Crown land used by the big lumber companies to shelter log booms. Logged off in the twenties, the debris of that exercise is still in evidence. It has been abandoned to summer camps and yacht club destination sites, with private cottages along the accessible bits of shoreline. Its oldest and only permanent centre of habitation is accessible by foot ferry from Gibsons, but every other traveller arrives by private boat or water taxi. The large ferries headed for Gibsons dump their wakes on it as they pass, but most Lower Mainlanders seem oblivious to this rocky, mountainous hand with its long fjords, cupped in the Howe Sound basin.

One summer when the third baby was almost walking, we rented a cabin there in an old settlement at the end of a decaying government pier. It was a time of pure family idyll, a storybook holiday. For me it was the fulfillment of some primal dream of home and my first experience of a different quality of living, outside of chronological time. I now name this quality, island or kairos, time. Outside of the impositions of clock and calendar, the rigidity of things falls away. The day becomes large and empty—something fluid, textured, and ambiguous to be filled with anything and nothing. When to eat, when to sleep, when to light the lanterns, when to come in, when to make fire, make love, play, sleep, talk, walk—all determined by desire or its absence. The day sculpts itself beyond human control around suddenly astonishing forces, like the rise and fall of tides, the patterns of weather, or the shifting exchange of light and dark. The falsely-generated needs and wants of urban life fade away in a gradual shift from lifestyle to living. The sojourner on an island isn't conscious of this paradigm shift, but something gets in under the skin, and she is never quite at home on the mainland again.

An acre of this island that drowses like a sleeping dragon along the Sunshine Coast amidst astonishing glaciers and snowy peaks became our summer home. Fifteen years after arriving on the coast I had found my way into the B.C. Book. We were weekenders, summer people. Even so, I was no longer a pilgrim but a settler, with proprietary rights and responsibilities. Although my new contractual relationship with this landscape was a luxury, its pleasures were hard won and had little to do with ease or money. Arrivals and departures were always uncomfortable, often difficult, and sometimes dangerous, each passage negotiated with anxiety and relief. With our young children, boxes and bags of groceries and all the accoutrements of daily living, plus whatever building supplies or bits of furniture we needed to replicate something like a house, we would cross the unpredictable five kilometre expanse of Howe Sound in an open boat, dodging the hotel-sized BC ferries and their wakes, arriving in our small bay only to have to pass everything from boat to dingy and row the last 100 metres to the beach. Huge tides, ferry wash and the notorious Squamish winds out of the north were often contenders for our safe arrival. I never got used to it.

My body, so familiar with the motion and rhythm of small boats in water, resists it still. The adrenaline floods of terror as the boat planes and plummets, pulling us through the unstable miles. Always there is the grey-blue question of survival and the possibility of being entirely taken over by fear. Horizons shift, islands loom and fade, debris makes an obstacle course out of any trajectory. I have learned that it feels better to stand and take the shock of waves through my feet. I am learning to lean into it more, to allow for groundlessness.

This island life I have been drawn to is punctuated by exits and arrivals, none of which are ever the same, ever comfortable, ever without the possibility of disaster. Yet sometimes I have felt the moment in which terror slips away and exhilaration begins, when the wave crests and holds for just a moment before the spume curls and begins its downward dive. In that instant lately I have felt myself submit to joy, to the wildness, to the ongoing uncertainty, as if happiness is permissible, even here. But mostly I love the arrival and its illusion of solidity. Blessed sand and rock, tree limb, shells, blessed shore. Arrival feels like victory, and although it takes a few hours to regain aplomb and a sense of balance, like childbirth, the memory of the terror quickly fades and I find myself doing the unthinkable again.

I don't really know what faith is, but I know how to leave the safe shore and ride the waves in acrobatic feats of hope, pleading for mercy all the way. And I know how to jump off on the other side, quickly, with a child in one hand and a bag in the other. With much practice the arrivals are becoming more graceful, the departures less ambivalent.

I don't know when I first became aware of it, but a phrase (which must have been part of a popular song at some earlier time) began to form itself as soon as I stepped onto the beach and took in my first breath of forest fragrance—*see me, touch me, feel me, heal me* it chanted. At every crossing this mantra found its way to the surface of my consciousness and I whispered it, like a pilgrim returning to a shrine where previous blessings had been dispensed and received. As I stooped to search for the sea's latest deposits of polished glass shards among the tidal debris on my spit of sand, I found myself wanting to submit to something. Like a mendicant with a bowl, I held myself out to earth, air, fire and water, and received what was given.

For the first years while the children roamed and my partner built a cabin, I slept. But it was more like a drowning in silence than anything resembling the sleep on the other shore of my life. I lay down on the beach and slept with a book on my chest and an eye on the children in the water. I slept on the forest floor wrapped in a blanket with deer browsing around me. I slept on the mossy beds of glacial rock behind the cabin, in a hammock slung between cedars, on the platform bed before the fire. I slept like a child returning home to her own bed after being in a strange place. When I emerged from this deep and profound sleep that lasted for several years, I had sloughed off the layers of accumulated weariness brought on by the struggles with marriage and family, professional development, studies, all the business and complexity that is scripted for women making their way in this world.

I awoke first to a sense of my own aliveness—the body electric, returning. Then to a presence abiding in the silent places of green upon green, a presence which cast a patina of sacredness over things. I awoke to a deeper awareness of what was and had been going on around me. Cracks and fissures appeared in the patterns of everyday life, revealing troubling disjunctures. I moved from the state of simple dependence and nurture into unfamiliar terrain again, looking for a new language to articulate experiences that were not mapped in to inherited structures of thought and faith. My body raged with hormonal dissonance and I was stunned by difficult relationships within and without. My days were full of work and my nights full of terror, the large questions of home and identity asking themselves again. Again I was wave-riding, jettisoning accumulated baggage, finding myself flung onto rock, wading out into deep water, hoping to come ashore at last, doubting always until the last second that I would arrive. And yet I did.

Always the genius loci of the island were there, accessible in body memory even when I was far from Gambier. I could find my way to the island in my mind and rest there, rocking in its mossy laps, bathing in the sweetness of salal and arbutus, ocean spray and cedar. I could hear the rush of the raven's wing across the clearing, the raucous greetings of gulls and eagles. I glimpsed the slick brown fur of the mink along the cliff's edge, caught the phosphorescence as it mocked the stars on a soft August night. Underneath it all, I could sense the abiding surge of surf, constant yet never still. I began to know I was loved. New sources of energy, creativity and joy emerged. The acre of rain forest on Gambier became my new address. The Ancient Presence in this second-hand wilderness, which changes so imperceptibly from year to year while always recreating itself, became distinctly She. I learned the word *pan-entheist* and applied it to myself. Everything here resonated with spirit, with meaning, with its own life. I marvelled and built altars on my sacred sites—circles of stones to which I brought humble offerings—returning to the gestures of my child-self, the cycle complete.

Light, dark, sound, silence, tide, wind and water are my unteachers. I learn to bear the beauty, to submit to silence as to joy, to tolerate the ambiguity of half-light or the unvarying remittance of green. I unlearn the craving for variation and the cold comforts of a small-scale world. My soul does swell again, even after long confinement, and the vigilant fifty-year old finds a self that fits; after much has fallen away, much remains. A breeze spinning maple leaves as they fall like dinner plates signals change; whitecaps in the bay suggest moving on; the tide's hourly in and out plays within a larger cosmic cycle of remove and return. I am simply here, awake and alert, where the sheltered moist places are, where water seeps perpetually out of the earth onto velvet mosses and galaxies of microbes break everything down and reform it again. I know I have come for benediction, begging absolution, yearning to be home.

Lately, I am coming to know myself here in yet another way. My being here at all is the result of privilege, which in turn, calls for accountability to the larger community. Our way of life on this island may be coming to an end as the machinery of progress makes its way here. A forestry conglomerate is even now plotting to remove the last groves of old growth trees. Without political will and the intervention of those who love it, this wilderness may disappear into what has come to be acceptable as the only remaining alternative—a managed recreation area, with easy access, electricity, and all that goes with it. Loss of connection to the wildness that remains, in this place where the immanent and transcendent intersect, would be an inestimable loss. This jot of an acre in the rain forest at the edge of a spreading metropolis is a microcosmic world of historic, biological and evolutionary processes that contain the seeds of our regeneration.

Here I can begin again to love, to revive hope and to finds the roots of justice and mercy. Only from here can I find my way back into the larger community of the earth. *This* particular island, *this* watershed, *this* biome of rock, sand, moss and tree, is *me*. The source of all that is to come is right here, in this blue-green place, which is not mine and yet profoundly so.

From the Gut

Rebecca Campbell

You'll go crazy inside so
open the door a crack, just for the blue mist of a comet.

Try a return to firelight and incandescence—
too late no escape from what hangs at the zenith
the splinters starlit hooks and tangles a pinwheel sky
that disintegrates and re-forms.

Inside what catches hair what wriggles
in through doorcracks down the chimney?
Outside again inevitably
the stars are barbed they tether your body
to the sailing moon leave the dark un-colour
of fresh blood in moonlight

And you swung up to the sky your body kaleidoscoped
disobedient and inside-out heart escaped
lungs long-gone skin slit at jaw and forearm by fish-hook stars

It's only a hint of what might-be.
Back here on earth there's a whisper:
                    remember and preserve your mind
                    against what will emerge.

Stirring the Cup

Dianne Linden

It snowed hard during the night, tiny recriminations of ice that gradually took up positions against me in my small house. At 3:00 AM the wind came up, ragged and determined, bearing news directly from the Arctic. I know this because I couldn't sleep, and got out of bed to keep myself company. It was then I looked out and saw how the snow had drifted around my back door to make an accusing finger and point it directly at the spot where I stood hunched over the kitchen sink, sighing and eating an orange. "I'm doing all I know to do," I said, crunching down on a bitter seed I hadn't known was there. "What difference do I make, anyway? What's the use of anything I do?"

I took fair-trade, decaffeinated coffee out of the freezer, measured it into an unbleached paper filter, added spring water and started the coffee maker. Something I had seen or heard recently was probably keeping me from deep sleep. Again. But what? There is so much to be wakeful about: the news that near Yellowknife men are once again penetrating the earth in search of her secret treasures; a CBC special on the end of the family farm; the article in the back pages of the newspaper about threats made against farmers who refuse to use genetically altered seeds. Tornadoes. Forest fires. Holes in the ozone layer.

Pain and disaster surround us. I confess I take it personally.

I try to lessen the impact of my lifestyle on the environment and those creatures I share it with. I stopped eating lobster long ago when I heard one being boiled alive. I quit eating veal after I learned how baby calves are isolated from their mothers and force-fed milk and hormones to keep their flesh white. Now the only meat I eat is fish and I'm working on that. I exercise conscience in what I purchase. I reduce, recycle, and reuse. Every year I take out more of the sod that surrounds my house and add flowers or vegetables. I trap rainwater in barrels for the garden. I don't use pesticides. I compost. I bless the wind and sing to it even when it beats down my delphinium.

Still, I admit that my North American existence is burdensome to the Earth. All that I do lacks boldness. And however much I try, I acknowledge that it is not enough.

By the time I poured my coffee, the wind and snow had settled down to rest around my house. I stirred skim milk and honey into the cup and carried it back to bed with me. Maybe it was the sudden quiet outside and the peace it brought, or simply the comfort and grace of homely rituals, but lying back against the pillows, my hands warmed by what they held, I became aware of the shape my stirring had given to the darkness in my coffee cup.

There was a milky spiral there now; a glimmering, white nebula that held its shape even while it shifted its position with the turning of the cup in my hand. It was then I realized the arrogance of the question I had thrown out into the storm. *What difference do I make? What's the use of anything I do?*

If the simple stirring of milk into coffee could create such eminence within the plainness of my cup, how could I ever know the outcome of any action, practiced with intention and from the heart? I lay awake a little longer, thinking how pointing fingers may simply be invitations to learn, thinking how important stirring is in the homely process of creation. And all that time the galaxy in my coffee cup glowed softly and held its own opinions.

Night Vision

Joanna Weston

Go out at night
to a clear view of sky

lean
against a rock

fill yourself with the dark
let it move into you

then turn the stars
outward—

you will have light
for the journey

V
From Generation To Generation

Born through the cycles of seasons
each generation from those gone before,
deep in awakening seedlings
the essence, the soul of the tree

We Shall Release A New Justice
Carolyn McDade

We Shall Release a New Justice

High on the ledge of the moun - tain Lim-ber and tall in the val - ley be - low Firm by the ri - vers on - flow - ing Faith - ful the trees ev - er stand. We, we shall re - lease We shall re - lease a jus - tice root - ed and deep, a tree spread-ing branch - es green and strong o'er all the earth, o'er all the earth.

We Shall Release a New Justice

Carolyn McDade

High on the ledge of the mountain,
limber and tall in the valley below,
firm by the rivers on-flowing,
faithful the trees ever stand

Born through the cycle of seasons,
each generation from those gone before,
deep in awakening seedlings
the essence, the soul of the tree

We, with the trees ever greening,
holding each child, a leaf to the sun,
praising within each emerging
our essence, our soul is one

We, we shall release
We shall release a justice rooted and deep
a tree spreading branches green and strong
o'er all the earth,
o'er all the earth

We Shall Release A New Justice: A Reflection

Elaine Mann

Reflecting on the lyrics of this song, it occurred to me that the title carries within it the essence of Carolyn McDade's life work, or at least what I have been able to grasp of the wisdom and inspiration of her music.

WE: Authentic community and solidarity are essential. To live respectfully and with deep gratitude for all of those who have gone before us is to enable and empower the existence of community.

SHALL: There is tremendous power in living and singing with intention, integrity and purpose.

RELEASE: We hold the creative energy and capacity to free each other and ourselves from oppression.

A NEW: The greening of the grass and the cycle of the seasons remind us of our connectedness with all of creation and teach us about possibility, persistence, faith and hope.

JUSTICE: When we act in solidarity and with intention, we create the possibility of a world in which all life is honoured and respected.

May this song be sung often and from the heart, giving each word the energy it deserves!

fossils waiting

Cathy Hodgson

think of me as layer after layer
of muskeg and permafrost
tribal evidence of pine and birch
ptarmigan and black bear
glacier becoming river
once at odds in the war of weather
now sunk to heavenly heat
think of me as lava hearted
with veins of gold
and teeth of diamonds
where wild strawberry
and bone of arctic wolf
have hardened their stories
to quartz coal silver
fossils waiting

Thanks to Di Brandt's Prairie Love Song

This Land Eats Things

Kerry Mulholland

This land eats things, devours them whole.
The innocence of prairie grass is pure deceit -
beneath those tender stalks, below roots' white fingers,
beyond the water they grope for, under that are bones.
Buffalo bones. Human bones. Blackened bones of dinosaur.
This land has eaten an entire sea—it is a carnivorous breadbasket.

We think we own some of this: there's evidence in a photograph.
You and me, younger, thinner (you still had that leather jacket).
Our smiles before a *sold* sign. Our house, our first, our piece of this soil.

Shrugging at our presumption, this land is. Ask the buffalo.
We'll tumble into it, sooner or later, our house will dissolve or fall,
our photographs rendered meaningless by earth, by wind.
While we join the rest of the bones and nourish the dirt,
prairie grasses will do ballet for the sky.

Next Year Country

Ardith Trudzik

Mummy can do anything. At least she does everything on our farm in the bush-country of northern Alberta. She's intelligent. And pretty, with fine bone structure and an energetic way of walking. She doesn't tell anybody about her health or her age. Or that we haven't any money.

Times are tough during the Great Depression, but Mummy and Daddy never take the dole. Daddy is a devil-may-care fellow with twinkly eyes and a hearty laugh. We're a happy family.

Then in 1939 our home catches on fire. Daddy sees smoke seeping through the shingles. Boards burn and crackle. Heat flushes my face as I stand on the step where Mummy thrusts a pan of stuff into my arms. "Dump it and run back with the pan."

I run to the woodpile, where Noël sits crying, "Get the dolls." Mummy has wrapped her snug as a cocoon in her blanket to prevent her from running back into the burning building. I dump my load of dishes and little jars of jelly beside her. Run back.

"Don't come in," warns Mummy. "The roof might cave. Here's another load."

Doug is carrying panfuls too. Ruby helps Daddy pull out the crib and sewing machine.

Sparks float like fireflies in the updraft. Our neighbours see the smoke and arrive in time to lug out the piano as flames leap from the windows.

Sealers full of raspberries and blueberries are strewn like broken beads across the snow, and we stand among them watching the house collapse.

Daddy glances around our yard, his eyes lighting on a granary, 14 x 16 feet, standing on skids. "We'll fix that up," he speaks in a husky voice. "It'll do temporarily. We'll build next year."

They set up our cabinet and cookstove. Its pipe turns outdoors through a sheet of tin covering a crude hole in the wall. They put in a window, build a strong door and nail a bunk across the entire back wall. Mummy stuffs ticks with straw and tosses up our quilt and pillows. She tells Noël and me, "Up on the bunk."

"How can we reach?"

She takes my cold hand. "Step on the chair. Stand on the table. Hop onto the bunk."

I shrink back. I'm not allowed to put even my elbows on the table. How can I put my feet there?

"It's warmer," she urges. "Help pull Noël up."

We huddle under the quilts while Daddy makes an orange-crate cupboard under the bunk for the home canning. He pushes under the sewing machine and crib. "Doug will have to sleep in the crib," he says.

"Save a crate for the washstand," says Mummy. "And an apple box for the firewood."

Our neighbours load our piano into their sleigh to store at their house. By nightfall we are settled. "Let's call this place the cabin so it sounds cosy," Mummy says, but her eyes are bleak.

***

More bad news. World War II breaks out. Daddy goes, promising, "I'll send home as much money as I can for our new house." He kisses us and as the steam swirls around us, he swings onto the train. We wave until he's gone. We're left with hearts like stone. Mummy turns away acting brave but her chin is wobbling. Her world has humpty-dumptied.

Back in the cabin she gives us scissors and an outdated T. Eaton and Company catalogue to cut paper dolls. Noël and I play paper dolls on the bunk, or press an eggcup into the frosted windowpane to make faces of fairytale people: Snow White, the wicked witch, Hansel and Gretel, Beauty and the Beast. Mummy tells their stories as the winter grinds through.

At last icicles drip from the cabin roof and the snow melts. Crows caw in the shelter belt, and ravens make dark shadows as they glide overhead.

When pussy willows burst from the branches we pull their furry knobs. Mummy's eyes go soft when we show her. "Would you like to make fur coats for your paper dolls with those?"

"Oh, yes."

She mixes flour-and-water paste.

***

That spring Mummy drives the Ford tractor to cultivate and seed the land. We trace her progress by watching white seagulls circling above her rig and listening for the whine of the engine. Her face is drawn and blackened when she comes in. Ruby serves squab pie. We seldom buy meat because Mummy's squirrelling money to have a new house built.

She hires men to trench a basement and make wooden forms for a foundation using a team and fresno. We watch them from a safe distance while we're seeding the garden with Mummy. The soil looks like a grey quilt staked to the ground at the ends.

She pours cement into the wooden forms; one-batch-at-a-time slops from the hand mixer. This job takes all summer. "Don't play here," Mummy warns, her face a white mask from the cement dust. "You might fall into the fresh cement." She tells us about Roman soldiers building walls with the bodies of slaves encased inside. We shudder at the thought.

An early snowfall stops this work. Mummy's eyes are wistful as she says, "It's too cold now, but we'll build next year."

Another winter in the cabin. Mummy keeps the cookstove burning but never quite conquers the blades of cold that creep under the poorly-fitted door. She pastes catalogue pages over the worst cracks. Every evening she scans our walls with the kerosene lamp, holding it under each bedbug until it loses its grip and falls into the flame to sizzle and die. Their stench is awful.

***

Flocks of Canada geese fill the sky with joyous sounds heralding the coming of spring. Mummy shows us the difference between the fragile buttercups and the hollow stemmed marigolds, between quivering aspen trees and Balm of Gilead, between pretty poisonous dogwood berries and tart high-bush cranberries, between warty toads and striped frogs, between robins' mud nests and orioles' woven hanging baskets. The steaming slough hums with mosquitoes but she sets a smudge outside our cabin door so they don't eat us alive.

Mr. McGee, the mason, builds a three-storey-high brick chimney, frightening me by howling down it like a banshee. He explains to Mummy that he's checking to be sure it draws well. Mummy counts coins into his hand.

When she saves more money, she hires Mr. Hill to build a two-story shell on the foundation. It looks funny with no doors or windows, but Mummy says, "I don't want rain to warp the lumber." As she saves more money, he returns to cut in one window and set the glass. Later he sets another.

Ruby uses a length of building paper to make folders with separate pockets for each of our paper dolls. We draw floor plans for their houses, arranging cut-out furniture. Our paper dolls have wonderful adventures on the bunk.

Visiting neighbours click their tongues, "How do you do it, Edith?"

We hold our breath, waiting for Mummy's reply. "I can't descend into self-pity. I have to rise above it." She turns to us with pride. "I have my family to raise."

Later she steps outside, taking in the sweet green smell of the fresh air and watching the swallows swooping over the corral. "As long as I have breathing space," she tells us, "I can face things."

Mummy picks our velvety raspberries, sour black currants, and crisp cabbage heads. She churns butter and presses it from her pound-mould onto wax paper, and gathers the fresh eggs. All these things she sells in town.

When the leaves turn golden and frost darkens the pumpkin vines, it's time to gather the neeps and tatties. The empty garden looks like an unmade bed. We see Mummy's pride in our new house. It stands like a castle on the hill. "It's not lined, and we've no furnace," she gives a grim smile. "But wait till next year."

We hear her treadle the sewing machine late at night. "There's a war on," she reminds us. "We must all make-do."

Doug uses scraps of lumber to make toys. We play war with these tanks and airplanes. Christmas gifts are scant, but we get a game of Snakes and Ladders to play with on the bunk.

Spring is welcome. We count snow geese in the cool sky, and hear the muttering of ducks nesting in our slough. "We'll plant a bigger garden," Mummy announces. "You can all help." She bends over the moist soil, her hands tender as she transplants cabbages. Her smile is tender, too. We know she's thinking of all the money we'll have when we sell some of the vegetables.

Mr. Hill starts shingling the roof, but the job is boring to watch. Noël and I search for a cool place. The mud in the pig wallow is twisted like black licorice, and the overhanging willows protect us. We fail to notice the dark clouds forming and glance fearfully at one another when the first few hailstones rattle across the ground, startling us with their coldness. Should we stay under the big cottonwood or run for the house? We head out, but are caught full-force. Hail bruises us, slicing our skins. When lightning sizzles, there's a smell like sulfur matches. We're lost in a summer blizzard. Running blind, we almost overshoot the house, but Mummy guides us in. She pats our flesh, the towel a huge cotton tongue lapping our welts.

"We have a great deal to be thankful for," Mummy claims. "Mr. Hill finished shingling the whole roof so no water leaked in except for this corner of the veranda wall where the exposed building paper has been torn to shreds."

"And I wasn't struck by lightning," Mr. Hill laughs. "I felt pretty close to God up there, I can tell you!"

"But our barley's gone, so I won't be able to buy a furnace. That means we can't move in till next year." Mummy's voice is choked.

"Now, Mrs. Ray, that's too bad." Mr. Hill shakes his head. "But right now I need a big chunk of building paper to repair the hail damage. Got any more?"

Mom draws us aside. "Girls, we have no more building paper except . . ."

"I guess you need our paper doll folders and house plans," Ruby says. "I'll move my family into a shoe box."

I eye Noël. "We will too."

Mr. Hill completes the main floor and blocks the opening to the upstairs of our new house. A neighbour helps him move in the cookstove and table. Mummy boils all our clothing, towels and bedding in strong lye soap, determined that no bedbugs hitch a ride into our new house. Doug doesn't need to use the crib any more. He's eleven years old and at last he can stretch full-length in a proper bed.

The neighbours come with a huge parcel wrapped in old quilts in the back of their wagon.

"My piano!" Mummy cries as tears make her eyes sparkle. We tug off the wrapping.

"Play for us," we beg.

She sits thoughtful for a moment, before striking the ivory keys.

> Have we trials and temptations?
> Is there trouble anywhere?
> We should never be discouraged—
> Take it to the Lord in prayer.

"Four years since we've had a decent house. Thank God we're home at last."

Watch the Creek

Brenda Schmidt

Spread the legs of the prairie,
sweat beading on spear grass,
panting as wind
stokes tight muscles,
whispers in her ear.

Slip in the crevice
surrounded by skin pocked
with cow parsnip, angelica,
poison hemlock to finally
find she is fully dilated.

Nod to the sky
blue blooms of speedwell
reflecting stems on the coming
waters that guide
as she begins to push.

Departures

Ruth Cey

I. December

Little one, born into diminished days,
you surrendered warm vibrant darkness to howling winds
that would tear breath from your nostrils.
Safe home, bundled blankets will not extend womb-life.

Too soon, on bleak, icy mornings, you will step out alone,
strain to see school bus headlights through fog,
their sweeping light catching coyote eyes in the caragana hedge.

I nurse you by the fire, to bathe you in light and warmth,
provisions for your wintry journeys ahead.

II. February

Midnight: swirling snow cloaks streetlights.
I pause at the intersection,
not trusting the back roads or wailing storm
with my baby,
I retreat to my mother's house.

She welcomes us, sleepily stirs the fire
and brings blankets to the living room,
now a temporary bedroom for my grandmother,
who wakens, confused by our late arrival
and probes the semi-darkness
with frail fingers outstretched.

I touch her hand;
she relaxes, reassured.
Blue-lines in her transparent arms and face
merge with bed sheet patterns.
But still her eyes are smouldering peat fires
of her northern homestead
that burn deep under winter snowbanks,

sending up clouds of damp smoke
to hang, wolf-like over white surfaces.
Clouds, stretched and shredded by wind until
only thready traces of fire's breath remain.

Grandmother sees the baby, smiles
then drifts to sleep, her questions answered.

Awake, I witness firelight's prophecy.
Sparks of trapped summer sun
light the baby's face and fattened folds,
throw shadows over blankets
that swath Grandmother's slightness
revealing what is no longer there.
Now hollows and cavities,
she has shed all but essentials
for the departure.

Outside, winds cease,
stillness settles over this midnight
intersection.

III. May

Early morning, startled awake by the telephone,
scattered sensations
damp breeze; warm rain filters sunlight;
dog bark sends sparrows
fluttering; a voice on the line.

Her departure was silent
soft, in sleep;
darkness devoured, her winter conquered.

Little one, I hold you, promise
I will tell you of the path she blazed,
sparks through stubble
clearing ground for new growth.

Birthing

Gayle Smith

It's dark. I awake, bump quietly in the night for clothes left handily
bedside. I slip them on, trying to keep the warm envelope of sleep
around me. Moving out to the kitchen my body is slow, disrupted
from its sleep. I lean against the wall, first one leg and then the other
coming to life as I crawl into my chore clothes.

Out in the night the stars shine overhead. I crunch along to the corral
where the heifers sleep. The subject of my attention is standing tail
out but not kinked, looking only mildly restless. I think she'll calve in
the morning. Hunched against the cold I trudge back to my snug bed,
shed chore clothes and put on sleep.

I awake to the dark morning and hear my husband talking about
calving as he starts the coffee perking. I put on my bedside clothes
and blink into the kitchen. I was right, the heifer has started. I pull on
my chore layers, going through the warming ritual again. The heifer is
in the barn, waiting. I shed my down coat and in short sleeves clean
her hind end off with warm water. I see two feet poking out through
membranes as she contracts. The sack is tough and I fish my hands
through warm folds of birth to slip calving chains up around the
fetlock joint of the calf. I'm getting warm, no longer notice the cold.

Seeing with my hands, I feel for life. A tongue moves. Good, it's alive.
Is there room? Yes. She should deliver without too much assistance.
The heifer pushes, mooing through the contraction. Methodically I slip
on the chains. The calf slips out, hanging head down. I clear its nose,
watching birth fluids drain away. It shakes its head and another
contraction slips it softly to the ground. A quick check shows me it's
a heifer too. The young mother looks intently at me. I back away and
she goes to her wet mass of life. She licks away and *mothering up* has
started.

Back in the house I wash and slip on city clothes for a city job. I
groom myself carefully, wondering if I still smell like birthing. The smell
of the barn is strange in my neat little office, but sometimes it trails
after me, leaving whiffs of memories.

The sun is rising as I wheel the car out of the yard. The morning colours are rich as the winter sun lights my way to the city. In my office of tranquillity I listen people's stories into new life. They tell me their burdens of sorrow, confusion and pain. I nod, I question, and we talk. In the back of my brain I'm thinking of birthing a calf, the tough membranes, the intensity of life, the relief of a breath taken, the awe of being there. As I focus on the present, I search through the folds of life, looking for a finger-hold on hope. I find an opening and start to tease out a new idea, a new vision, a new way of responding. My heart feels warm with love as a story of hope emerges. Someone listens, another experiences relief. Insight blossoms. A new way to walk through life is born.

My day in the city over, I review it in my head. I feel drained and disorientated. A pattern of emerging life reveals itself. I think about the sweet heifer calf. My feet feel the ground again as they crunch through the snow to the barn. I see her curled up in the clean straw, warmed by the heater hanging above her. Her large liquid eyes peer out of a beautiful face. What a wonderful day. Amen.

Lee's Hands

Denise Needham

This woman's hands have experience. When they were 55 years old, they learned to mesh gears in a Russian tractor, work with left foot on clutch, right foot on brake, turn around and lever down to make the bucket go up. Ahhhhh! She's like a ballerina—so smooth. Poetry in motion. The diesel engine is like music to her ears. Her fingers tighten a connection on a hydraulic hose—another damned leak—fluid drips and runs down her arm to her elbow through the smear of axle grease. A swipe of her forehead to whisk off a fly leaves a trail down her cheek.

These same hands at -30°C spread the vulva lips of an anxious heifer and released a hot wet calf to the world. They stroked and squeezed teats and started new milk to run—rich yellow colostrum like sweetened condensed milk—sticky fingers eagerly sucked by a rough tongue.

Eight years ago about this time of year Lee took up with me and experienced something not unlike our Russian tractor, a loud, noisy body of parts requiring massaging, tweaking, lubing and fluid checks. I swear she's just as much at one with me in bed as she is with her tractor.

the making

Lia Pas

hands inside
of leaves . of feeling . of pots . of dirt

hands turning dark with the mud of the earth
songs and voices moving meatily out through this tongue
lips full of lemon's sweet bleach

keep the hands busy
rub soil over milky breasts
feel the warm life start like a small taste

        like the moon's blood
        like the sounds made in love making

        dark and pungent with a scent of sweet

Metamorphosis

Lois Kennedy

When the caterpillar weaves its cocoon, imaginal disks begin to appear which contain the blueprint for the future butterfly. Although these new disks are produced by the caterpillar's own body, its immune system recognizes them as foreign and begins to attack them. However, as more disks are produced and begin to congregate, the caterpillar's immune system is overwhelmed and its body begins to disintegrate. As the disks mature into imaginal cells, they arrange themselves into a new pattern. In this way the disintegrating body of the caterpillar is transformed into a butterfly. The caterpillar has not actually died because from the beginning its destiny was to transform into the butterfly.

I am an embryologist, so this is familiar territory. Embryologists concern themselves with life's earliest stages of growth and development. Dealing as it does with miraculous physical transformations such as the one just described, it is a science that is rich with analogies and insights about transition and transformation in the non-physical realms of both our inner emotional and spiritual evolution and our outer social and cultural evolution. In retrospect, it was probably my love of metaphor, mystery and the miraculous which drew me into this science, rather than any particular interest in becoming a scientist.

Mother Nature has surprisingly few ways at her disposal to create and respond to change. There are a limited number of patterns that form common threads through all forms of evolutionary change, whether they be in the physical biological world or the non physical social/spiritual world. The story of the imaginal disks illustrates the biological processes of cellular induction and migration that underlie the formation of virtually every physical feature or organ system of every life form on the planet. Similar patterns underlie the formation of wings and feathers, limbs, toes and toenails, kidneys, hearts and brains, the branches and leaves of trees, the buds of flowers . . . .The enormous diversity and complexity of life that we see around us is due mainly to the infinite ways the few basic patterns of growth and development can be expressed.

Similar patterns also underlie our emotional, spiritual and social transformations. Although I once regarded one to be a metaphor for the other, I now see this as my own failure to recognize that common patterns are present in all types of metamorphosis. Naming a biological process as a metaphor for my spiritual or social metamorphosis implies that they are somehow separate or different aspects of my evolution as an individual. This was a reflection of an anthropocentric worldview, of our culture's insistence on seeing the natural or physical world as other-than ourselves. Recognizing that these common patterns underlie all aspects of our personal and social metamorphosis may help us to develop a more holistic approach to our evolution as individuals and as a society. It may provide the framework for taking conscious control of our evolution. It may help us initiate changes in our way of living in community and on the earth that can influence our personal, social and planetary futures.

There are many lessons hidden in the story of the imaginal disks of caterpillars. One which I find of particular significance to our personal growth is the principle of learning to differentiate self from non-self. The caterpillar initially does not recognize the imaginal disks as self and blocks its own metamorphosis into its butterfly self. Often our own growth is stunted or blocked because we cannot differentiate between traits which are part of our true nature and those which we have internalized about ourselves from outside sources. Such things as negative cultural values and social pressures to be normal or nice may cause us to deny or repress characteristics which may actually be our best and most beautiful gifts. Criticisms and rejections might be accepted as truths and internalized as part of self. These can then act like an introject or a computer virus which is not part of the original programme, but can create problems. Our failure to recognize them as non-self causes such confusion that we block our own metamorphosis into our highest and most beautiful selves. Growing true to our own nature, becoming our butterfly selves, requires that we learn to recognize and overcome that within us which is non-self and then to honour and express that which is truly self.

Another developmental principle illustrated in the metamorphosis of the caterpillar is the important role of critical mass. In order for a major transformation from an old order to a new order to occur successfully, a critical mass of individuals with the new blueprint has to be assembled. Put another way, the status quo (the caterpillar) will prevail until the new order (the butterfly) is sufficiently evolved and coherent to succeed. The emergence of the butterfly would fail if the transformation were initiated immediately upon the arrival of the first one or two individuals with the new blueprint. However when a critical mass of the new cells is achieved, the caterpillar's immune system is overwhelmed and the new order, the butterfly begins to emerge. The caterpillar immune system's initial attack on itself is actually a survival strategy to ensure the ultimate success of the butterfly.

We follow this same strategy when we are facing a major change in our personal lives. Do we not prepare for it by carefully re-visioning our lives, or creating a new blueprint, and then surrounding ourselves with a group of like-minded friends to support us through the transition? This pattern is also seen in the process of major social transformation. Witness the imprisonment of Nelson Mandela, the assassinations of Gandhi, Martin Luther King Jr., and John F. Kennedy, or the brutal and ruthless persecution and harassment of women such as Fannie Lou Hamer and Rosa Parks. Were these not men and women whose visions and blueprints for a new social order were ahead of their time? Without a critical mass of awakened individuals to support them in their vision they were targeted as non-self by the status quo and attacked. Transformation was blocked, but only temporarily. As the number of people with the new vision increased and came together, the old order was overwhelmed and the transformation of society into the new order proceeded.

The world today is in deep pain, in the midst of the tumultuous process of transformation. It is no longer the old order but not yet the new order; it is a work-in-progress. But there is a massive paradigm shift occurring as people everywhere are awakening to the realization that our current way of living on the planet is economically, socially and environmentally not sustainable. A critical mass of people with a new social vision now exists and these people are coming together, transforming themselves and their cultures into a new order—a new way of being is emerging.

Over the last five years I have been engaged in a long process of deep personal transformation. I have been travelling in some very deep and dark places, in those liminal spaces, the unknown, un-named spaces between the caterpillar and the emerging butterfly. It is a journey which is at times fully conscious, engaged and purposeful, but which is also paradoxically filled with periods of confusion, uncertainty, despair and disequilibrium. It is the journey through the swamplands of the soul, an endless inner dialectic between the mind and the heart. It is being adrift on the ocean in a storm with no map, no life jacket and no shore in sight. I am in a constant struggle wanting to move forward to something radically new but wanting to wait until I can see more clearly what it is that I am moving towards - my faith and confidence are often over-stretched. Consciously working out the details of a new blueprint for my life (a fate spared the caterpillar) requires patience and insight. Some days faith, confidence, patience and insight all seem to fail at once. I understand Sam Keene's definition of faith as *dancing in the dark*—I would much rather be dancing in the light. If what the Buddhists say is true, that the two pillars of wisdom are paradox and confusion, then some day I will be a very wise old woman.

I am new to a group of women who have named themselves "Women of the Sacred Web." It is a community deeply committed to healing through song and action—the healing of our selves, the healing of our communities, and the healing of the earth. It is also a community in transition, in the process of re-visioning itself after the production of the compact disc *We are the Land We Sing* with Carolyn McDade. Many of my observations and comments about metamorphosis are in response to this community and our process of change.

There is another personal aspect to the healing and transformation I am experiencing within the Sacred Web community. Many of my deepest wounds and some of the biggest obstacles to my social and spiritual growth have come from women. I have come to realize that the wholeness I always sought in wilderness and the transformation I am now experiencing within the Sacred Web community is the attempt to heal these wounds.

In her book *The Bond Between Women: A Journey to Fierce Compassion*, China Galland expressed the experiences of many of us very well when she described how we constructed our worlds around those parts of ourselves which we had denied or cut off, how we anesthetized our pain, ignored our experiences and silenced our voices as we "tried to live discreetly within the closed system of male dominance." Undoing these cultural influences and bad bargains has been a large part of my need to go into the wilderness, to reclaim my true nature, to learn from other women.

As part of her discussion, China related the words and teachings of Michel Henry, part Cree, part Ojibway, part Irish, who returned to her reservation in her late forties to learn the lineage and teachings of women:

> The biggest betrayal has been women betraying
> women. Once the wound between women is healed,
> the wound between men and women can heal; once
> the wound between men and women heals, the
> family can heal; once the family heals, the community
> can heal; and once the community heals, the world
> can be healed. That's what the Grandmothers say . . . [2]

We must turn to women for healing, we must seek out our women elders to empower us, and we must together learn to affirm and nourish the fierce, sacred feminine within. Women's wisdom has its own inherent tradition of what it takes to make and sustain life.

China Galland concluded that "The wound is the space between us, where we kept ourselves apart, where we didn't talk, where we couldn't hold each other and cry."[3]

My experience of the Sacred Web Project is that it is an open community of women passionately committed to change, to a new way of being in the world which loves and respects women, the earth and spirit. I see us as part of the critical mass of awakened beings who can and will, through deep personal transformation, bring about conscious social and environmental evolution.

Understanding the patterns of the process of transformation provides a map, a guide through the darkness. Deep connections within the embrace of a healing community provides a life-jacket which buoys us on the waves of the storm. The depth of love and wisdom in Carolyn McDade's songs is the light shining on a distant shore, and our passionate singing together in community strengthens and sustains our faith and confidence that we can get there.

We are a disseminated tribe, but a tribe none-the-less. We come together to renew ourselves through singing, through sharing and reflection in community. Then we disperse and return to our home places to do the work each of us must do. Even when we are apart, there is wonderful sustenance in remaining connected to the healing energy and wisdom of this community of women by singing and by re-membering our gatherings. This is what we are all about, strengthening the bond between women, healing, re-visioning, and transforming ourselves and our communities and our way of walking on the earth. Our great blessing is not just the passion we experience in singing together, it is the new and compassionate culture that we are bringing into being for ourselves, for others, and for the healing of the planet. So be it.

---

[1] China Galland. The Bond Between Women: A Jouney to Fierce Compassion, New York: Penguin Putnam, 1998, 87.
[2] Ibid., p. 88.
[3] Ibid., p. 92

Learning to Read

Shirley A. Serviss

Women's history is written in
freehand beading on buckskin
jackets, patterns of even stitches
through patches and carded wool,
loops of cotton crocheted into lace.
It follows rules of even rows
of vegetables in gardens, jars of
preserves on pantry shelves,
washing hung to dry in the sun.

Women's history is telegraphed
in the rhythmic scraping of hair
from a hide, the turning of a
butter churn, the scrubbing
against washboard or river
stones. It is a code we have
not learned to decipher or
trained our ears to hear.

Women's history is darned
into socks, punched into
bread dough like letters of
Braille poked into thick paper
with a stylus. We are too blind
to read it. We miss the messages
written in recipe collections,
carved in the crusts of pies.

What Lasts

Sylvia Chetner

When my bones become prairie
I will remember
how the face of the land lies flat
under the big blue sky up above
how west the dinosaur spine
of the Rockies rises
purple and grey
and meeting the sky

When my bones become prairie
I will remember
how the breast of the foothills
rises and falls
how the wind sucks the badlands dry
leaving stones and coulees
and fingers of hoodoos behind

When my bones become prairie
I will remember
how banks of cumulous clouds
send shadow hulks scudding
across the swaying summer grass
how poplar sounds wash
in waves through the trees

When my bones become prairie
I will remember
how in summer, night disappears
and skylight lasts until morning
how in winter, days shrink
to fit the palm of the hand
and the sun seated on the horizon's rim
spins the air into gold

I will remember the land
I will remember
when the dust of my bones
blows free

bald hills

Christine Wiesenthal

back there, up on the brown bald hills
i shrugged off my bones for good

unclasped the spine
at the nape of the neck,
let clatter a string of vertebrae
a strand of pearls

collar undone, the remains crumpled
free, my head wedged in my wishbone
& cradled there, comfortably

the lattice of my limbs collapsed, in relief
some lucky knuckles & two
knee caps rolled

& crowning the top of the mound,
all this ribbed ivory debris

my hip bones still
sometimes rock

back there, up on the brown bald hills
my white bones lie for good

upstream

Linda Wikene Johnson

if you follow a river
upstream far enough
it turns green
and climbs mountains
eventually
you reach the bright sky
and feel
a crisp white evaporation
shaking up
to the sun

death must feel like that

❧

VI
Together We Rise

You carry my story,
I your truth and claim
Our lives a leaven to rise again

Uprising of Hope
Carolyn McDade

Uprising of Hope

A song for Leaven honouring their work in the areas of spiritual development, feminism, anti-racism, and sexual justice. They gather around this commitment: "If we would be as leaven, there could be an uprising of hope."

© 1998 by Carolyn McDade

O Sing-ing Cre - a - tion Ar-dent ar- ias of grace Dream swirl-ing in
O ri – ver of wa – ters O blos-soms of field Deer wan-der the

dark-ness un - furls a wide em - brace Earth, blue-land of wa - ters
su - mac as cy-cles reach and yield O cir- cle of an - cients

Long green-ing of soul Love stir-ring leav- en with - in the whole.
Come, ga-ther us in Los - ing each o -ther, our fall from dream

A ris - ing hope, a ris - ing of hope We as

lea - ven rais - ing an up - ris - ing of hope

Uprising of Hope

Carolyn McDade

O Singing Creation,
Ardent arias of grace
Dream swirling in darkness unfurls a wide embrace
Earth, blueland of waters
Long greening of soul
Love stirring leaven within the whole

O river of waters
O blossoms of field
Deer wander the sumac as cycles reach and yield
O circle of ancients
Come, gather us in
Losing each other, our fall from dream

Come bend to the river
Stones washing in rain
Love caught in the narrows will seize the stream again
Come bare to the meadow,
grass lifting the sun
All rise with morning creating dawn

A rising hope, a rising of hope
We as leaven raising an uprising of hope

Come, friend, I go with you
'yond the road and its end
Turn, soft through the meadow to round the river's bend
You carry my story
I, your truth and claim
Our lives a leaven to raise again

A rising hope, a rising of hope
We as leaven, raising, an uprising of hope

Who goes the journey
Whence cometh our strength
What all abiding is changed forever, changing
What stirred in our passion
to its witness is true
Where wakens wisdom and all made new

our lives made new
our love made new
our world new again

*The words of this song are rooted in the gathering commitment of
Leaven, an organization working in the areas of spiritual development,
feminism, anti-racism and sexual justice. "If we would be as leaven,
there could be an uprising of hope."

Uprising

Audrey Brooks

The sound of bubbling coffee
runs over spaces
between the echo
of our last notes
and the silence
before voices
sing again

We chant
we build, empower
give essence, glory
calling names of
sister
lover
mother
grandmother
daughter
friend

We ask
why sorrow
who can know
where is earth
what includes, deepens
defines, resonates

We know
songs of sorrow, of healing
of deep understanding
of women in community
of storytelling, of wisdom

We know
how to sing from inside a song
with authority for its meaning

Letter to Courtney

Diane Driedger

For many years the author has spent part of each year working with volunteer agencies in Trinidad and Tobago. While there she met a soul mate. Together they hiked beaches and rain forests. In this letter, she continues their conversation from Canada.

Dear Courtney,

I went for a walk today, thought about how the scenery is the same and different from the Caribbean landscape that we shared together when I visited Trinidad and Tobago. Today it is 27°C, a typical Winnipeg July day. I got ready for my walk—put on my orange Caribbean T-shirt and my brightly striped Guatemalan cap, jeans and Reeboks and popped a purple Popsicle into my mouth. I got into the elevator in my building and people looked at me.

Then I was out of the elevator, headed for Wellington Crescent. I saw flowers everywhere; red geraniums and orange marigolds, most of them clumped in solidarity. There wasn't even one weed in their midst, nothing to tear them asunder. Sounds biblical, doesn't it? I thought how wonderful that the flowers can be together and not lined up in straight rows. I remember how my mother used to plant her suburban flower beds always the same. She had small purple flowers lined up in the front, and then a middle row of red salvia and then the back row either yellow or orange marigolds. This was always the way they were lined up. I thought to myself how revolutionary to see these flowers breaking out of patterns, growing where they wish and even seeing a little purple flower peeking out from beneath some juniper hedges every once in awhile.

The air smelled of pine, flowers and freshly cut lawns as I walked along the curved road of Wellington Crescent to the park on the river. It's calm today, really unlike prairie weather. I thought of our visits to the beach in Tobago, waves a gentle in and out heartbeat, a breath. Here in Winnipeg, we have these hurricane-like winds that blow the trees continually, that make your ears hear rushing sounds like the ocean. But on this day there was only a slight breeze that caused the poplar trees on the other bank of the river to wave their sequins as the sun shone on them.

I stretched out on the riverbank and felt the grass. Once a friend told me that whenever she feels depressed she lies on "the ground of Mother Earth.' She lives in Victoria, B.C., so she can do this year round. But here in Manitoba I must do it now because it's July, a time when one *can* lie on the ground. Anyway, she lies on the ground and lets the earth support her. I realized when I was doing this that the energy of the ground seeped into my bones and I felt free of the back pain that has been with me for the last three years. I felt the curves of the earth like a futon molding around my body.

Ted once told me that camping was uncomfortable because the ground was hard and all in the wrong places. To me, every twig and root was in the right place today. On the water I saw the reflections of trees and the green bank of the other side of the river, and it made me think of Monet and his paintings of water lilies. You know, he painted those blurred water scenes in the last days of his life because he had cataracts. On this day I saw the same thing, my vision slightly blurred with the pleasure of soaking in the light around me. Trees, like sentinels, protected me. When I sat up I was much straighter. I felt my heart beating new energy through my veins, and my head was clear. It almost felt like I was back in the Caribbean on one of our rainforest hikes in Tobago.

The land is the same, wherever you are in the world, and not only good when it is warm and green. I used to be resentful towards this prairie landscape when those forty below winds in the winter threatened to blow me off the street. But somewhere under those snowdrifts, nature lives. Not only that, she *is* the snow. When you come to visit we must take a river walk, summer or winter.

Take care,

Diane

Catching Crows

Marian Shatto

*For years Carolyn McDade and I have referred to the process of
music notation as "perching crows on wires." The round fat bodies of
the notes, with stems and winged flags, take their places on the lines
of the staff, nestled within, hanging on below or flying freely above.
Music notation is a utilitarian craft, a means of providing a clear,
accessible path into the song. The notator works primarily in solitude,
but never in isolation. Her work is brought to the singing circle in
collaborative process—listen and write, listen and write. Here then is
the meditation of the notator.*

The multi-layered onion is often used to represent complexity of
meaning. As the surface is carefully removed, successive layers are
revealed, each with its own tangy richness. At the heart of the bulb is
that kernel which gave it birth.

Carolyn's songs, as they are sung into being, are something like that
onion. Text and melody are the kernel, her gift to the gathered
community. Notes like crows soar and dip, persuaded finally to light
upon the wires of the staff. Thick chords like sturdy tree trunks stand
tall with rooted support. Granted both roots and wings, the song
begins its journey into the world.

Sometimes a melody takes flight before it is wedded to text. The
instruments claim it and sing it in that language which is beyond
words. Oboe caresses a phrase, then tosses it to flute, who turns it
glistening an octave closer to the sun. Harp adds a cascade of sparkle,
while 'cello grounds the whole in rich, deep tones of earth. Piano
builds solid structure of rhythm and chord, providing the frame in
which the others may dance. Thus does the community of
instrumentalists weave its patterns into the web of song.

More often, though, voices of gathered singers begin to add layers to
the ripening song. Within this collaborative process it is sometimes my
joy and privilege to discover inner voice parts implicit in the deep-
rooted chords. Other times it is in the group singing that lines
emerge—weaving, soaring, grounding.

Startled by some surprising twist of melody, or joyously inspired by a turn of phrase, whole flocks of crow-notes may suddenly take flight, only to alight again in ever-shifting patterns on the staff. The songs are organic, living, endlessly variable. A recording of Carolyn's music is a snapshot, a record of one moment in time, but never the final word. Like life itself, there is no final word to this music, no granite carving which has relinquished the potential for growth and change. Each singer brings her own story, finds her own way of being with the song. And each group that gathers to sing weaves its own energy, adds its own strands to the sacred web.

Crows on wires become a road map, a guide into the song. They are suggestive, not definitive. There are always byways to explore, unmarked lanes yielding insight and delight. The song journeys out and returns wiser, more mature, calling the community to share again in its riches. Community and song together commit anew to the process—joy in creation, exuberance in discovery, and deep thanks for the blessing which is life.

Piecing It All Together

Martha Cole

I've been a practicing/producing/exhibiting artist for over twenty-five years. Most of that art production has been done working alone in my studio with varying degrees of insecurity. On occasion, I have worked on group projects of one kind or another. More recently, I have had a number of women working with me and helping me execute my larger scale fabric works. Mostly I've been ambivalent about collaborations, although I realized that creative group projects often produce final works that are very different (and often better) than the work of the individuals involved, myself included. With more recent works where other women were working with me, it was always *my* concepts and goals that we all directed our energies toward.

But in the summer of 1999, I joined with a group of women at the Banff Centre for the Performing Arts to assemble a quilt in a different way. The theme of the project was Women-Land-Spirit, and eighty-nine women were gathered to produce the recording, *We Are the Land We Sing* with Carolyn McDade. One of the other creative threads of this gathering was the production of a quilt with the same theme. It wasn't my vision, wasn't my *project*. I saw myself as bringing certain skills to an open-ended project encompassing an unknown number of women. The energy for the quilt came from a number of different women. It didn't draw on my creative vision only, which freed me to enjoy the creative process more than I ever had. I had a wonderful time!

Individual women would come into the room where we were assembling the quilt, take a look at the work in progress and say, "You need to put red in that spot," or "I think you need to add a band of Flying Geese across that area." They were absolutely right almost every time. And, when they weren't, someone else standing there would say, "Well, actually, I think . . ." and a discussion would ensue with each woman responding to what had already been said. Eventually we would get it right and then all we had to do was execute it.

Invariably, those solutions were so much more than anything I would have come up with if it had been left just to me with my single vision. Participating in this collaborative effort has permanently altered my core understanding of the creative process and it's relationship to community. The whole was so much more than the sum of all the parts.

I see my next step as moving these new understandings out of the specific Women-Land-Spirit quilt context and integrating them into the wider spheres of my life. The quilt has moved out into the world and I hope to do the same.

Fabric of the Spirit

Carol Breitkreutz

At a fortieth birthday retreat for a friend, I was introduced to a form of creative expression that has changed my life. At this celebration, my friend Mary Wilton led the gathering in the doll-making techniques she had learned at a summer workshop. Each of us brought cloth, yarn, and other embellishments that we shared in communally to make dolls for ourselves as well as something that could be incorporated into a special doll for the birthday person. I made a pillow doll, a guardian angel, to keep my son from restless nights. She still sits at his bedside, her cherubic countenance patiently watching over him.

Shortly after the birthday retreat, Mary and I began singing together regularly with a group of women who cared passionately about the land and expressed this passion in their singing and their living. In our earnest discussions after these singing circles, the idea of crafting dolls to represent different elements and aspects of the music emerged. We discovered the joy of creating dolls that are not only representations of human forms, but suggest a deeper spiritual connection. The dolls became a part of the visual and spiritual experience of our singing together as they joined us in our circle. They spoke to the women in these circles in different ways and soon became known as "Spirit Dolls."

Mary and I have each found our own unique ways of making Spirit Dolls, and each doll we have created is itself unique. For me, making a Spirit Doll begins as an impression in the back of my mind, sometimes inspired by the words and melody of a song, sometimes by emotions or ideas. Often the first aspect of the doll that I discern is the posture of the body. My Spirit Dolls are unlike other handmade dolls in the traditional sense of doll making. They are more impressionistic and abstract in their shape, designed to evoke an emotional connection with those who experience them.

The Earth Spirit Doll is sewn from grey and brown cloth that looks like the stones of a streambed. She is kneeling, head bowed, hands outstretched, caressing the earth with garden tools and small seed packets around her. The Fire Spirit Doll is red and gold, her hair like a fire silhouetting her head. She is dancing with her arms stretched over her head holding a crystal flame. Air is an elderly woman made of stormy sky material with wind-tousled hair, a sheet stretched high overhead, as she greets the storm while taking clothes off a line. Water stands erect, cradling shells and starfish in her arms, ripples of ribbon about her feet. Netting cascades and billows down around her head like sea foam on the tide. Searching for small objects that the dolls may hold, wear or have about them is a joyous treasure hunt. Miniature garden tools, clothespins, shells, crystals, stones, dried plants, flowers, pouches—all add to the character of the doll and often have symbolic significance.

There is so much beautiful fabric that represents the land, rocks, skies, vibrant flames, swirling waters, rolling hills, verdant forests—so many colours and designs that the possibilities are limitless. I have evolved into a person who loves the feel of cloth and the vibrancy of the designs and colours. Going into a fabric store is like taking a walk in a fragrant garden; all my senses are alert and my spirit sings. I become intoxicated with the possibilities of the medium.

Sometimes doll making can bring healing to wounded spirits. Mary led a doll-making workshop at the Cross Cancer Institute in Edmonton, Alberta, as part of that institution's Revlon Arts in Medicine program. Women experiencing various needs for the healing of their bodies, minds and spirits, learned how to create dolls to accompany them on their journeys.

For the first four decades of my life, my creative expression was muted, emerging occasionally with a flash and then dissipating. But in this fifth decade the focus has become sharper, the colours more intense and the expressions more varied. It has become a joy and a responsibility to take the yearnings and intentions of another and try to stitch them into a Spirit Doll that is unique for that person. It has also been an honour to lead others in the crafting of their own Spirit Dolls, allowing them to capture glimpses of their own spirituality through this process.

Sacred Space

Monica Rosborough

Creating a sacred space within my community involved careful preparations. I was surprised at how much paper was needed for this ritual—permits, site plans, exterior sketches, blueprints, and schematic diagrams. The gathering of people that was involved was intricate; community, committee, community, and back to committee to hone and perfect the dream. Talking to experts for their wise words was also important; architects, security advisers, electrical, mechanical and structural engineers, acoustic specialists, and kitchen designers. Then all the energy was channelled into a creative frenzy until construction was achieved and the space was completed.

I have been in many places that are called sacred. Some were heavy with thick spicy incense, chanting sing-song voices and large-eyed portraits of placid faces. Others were filled with stony, staring gargoyles and painted statues. Some were filled with a kaleidoscope of sun-stained colours from tall windows and uplifted ceiling, while others had the universe painted on a domed roof, with twinkling stars and artistic clouds. Some were built with rocks or oppressive columns that felt so cold that I shivered on a hot summer day. Some were fields empty of buildings but filled with a circle of singing dancers on a cool, midsummer's eve. Once I stood at an ancient circle of rock, older than the bones of my oldest known ancestor. It was littered with pop cans, wrappers, store flyers and filled with camera-clicking tourists but empty of soul-full magic. My heart has led me to a simple space where the circular dance of life is both celebrated and lamented by a community that feels like home.

I have also been tempted to make my own sacred space, imagining circles of candles, icons of wide-eyed serenity, talismans, hymns, herbs. Instead, I find that it is the unplanned and unorchestrated moments of life that are filled with meaning—the early dawn illuminating my lover's face as I wait for his first waking glance, the lapping of waves on a canoe heading for home, the appearance of an enormous hare on a wintry city lawn, a hammock with a good book, a rocking chair with paper and pen, a bunk bed at night holding a sleepy little boy. These, rather than bricks, coloured glass or flickering candles, are the most sacred spaces in my life.

Let the Dance Begin

Lois Smith

I let myself relax into the rhythm. Allow my body to rock gently back and forth. My eyes point the way as I float towards my destination. I circle around and pick up speed, keeping my shoulders straight and my hands soft. I am riding horseback and the dance has begun.

I had reached one of those plateaus in life where I knew instinctively that I needed to reach out and get back in step with my natural world and myself. It seemed that my world narrowed as I entered the productive years of child rearing and achieving work-related goals. My simpler self, my spiritual life was often put on hold or forgotten altogether.

I initially chose horseback riding as a way to exercise. I thought it would be fun and would hold my attention. It was a time in my life when I was feeling stressed from overwork and lack of empowerment in my life. While I enjoyed my family and busy professional life, it seemed I rarely had time or energy to pursue other interests. This decision was to change my life.

My first day at our local stable was exciting and bewildering. It was hard to know who was more nervous, my new friend Bud, or myself. Although it turned out Bud was an experienced school horse, my coach explained that the first meeting is always a little scary for the horse as he sizes up the new rider to see what kind of person he has on the hoof now. Once he realized he was a better horse than I was, his fears were over and mine just beginning.

Over the following months I learned to understand Bud and we became friends. He was patient when I made a mistake, which was often, and he always forgave me. I learned to balance myself on that small English saddle, using muscles I never knew I had. Bud walked me through all sorts of patterns; he was willing to teach me everything I needed to know if I would only learn to listen in horse language. It took me a while to learn it and until I did, my coach was the interpreter.

I made new friends with a number of other women, our common interest in animals forging a bond that lasts to this day. We learned together, helped one another and gradually became more competent in our quest. As more months went by I started to realize that I was smiling more and my clothes fit again. I stopped worrying about everything, and when I felt stressed I meditated with mental images of riding.

Although the years ahead brought their own trials and challenges, I remained grounded thanks to my involvement with horses and the spiritual peace that comes with working with other creatures. Horses live in my pasture now and I encourage other women to experience the wonderful feeling of empowerment that comes from riding a one thousand pound animal that actually listens to their every word. Of course every word they speak must be in horse language but it's fun learning to communicate in a new and exciting way.

A few years ago I developed a horseback-riding therapy program for women who wished to return to a more vigorous life. The program was born out of my love for these wonderful animals and a desire to share my experiences with others. The women who found their way to our farm initially came for fun and exercise; they left having gained much more than they expected, through their own efforts.

I remember one of the first riders who appeared at my door to inquire hesitantly if I thought she could learn to ride. Ellen was a heavy woman in her mid years who suffered from asthma and stiffening of her joints from osteoarthritis. She was struggling with change-of-life symptoms, and exercise made her hot and uncomfortable. As a result she lived a sedentary lifestyle, engaging in very little physical activity. She explained to me how much she loved horses and wanted to ride but found regular lessons intimidating. She wondered if she would ever be able to mount a horse because of her weight and poor physical condition; she was too embarrassed to try in public. My offer of individualized lessons brought her to my door.

From the beginning Ellen found solace in making friends with one of our sturdy, quiet geldings. She learned to groom and tack him, which meant brushing, cleaning and dressing the horse in his blanket, saddle and bridle. She was amazed to see him lift his feet for her so she could carefully clean his hooves to ensure no stones lurked in tender spots. She was able to climb on board with the help of a mounting block. Her new friend carefully planted his feet so he could stand steady while she shifted her weight onto his back. She learned that it is difficult for a horse to do this, and that it depended on the rider's skill in mounting rather than the weight of the rider. She determined that day she would learn to mount so that it wouldn't hurt her horse. She learned to put him first and he rewarded her with gentle patience.

Over the following months Ellen's balance improved and her body started to respond with increased muscle strength and flexibility. Mobility began to return to her joints and she started feeling better. She learned new skills she thought were beyond her grasp. She found a new vitality, and now when she goes dancing she and her partner float around our pasture and down the trails with smiles on their faces.

I have seen this experience repeated, with variations, by the many women who have found their way down our country lane. What wonderful gifts these horses offer us. By watching we learn to talk. By partnership we learn to trust. By letting go of ego we learn to share power. By caring we learn to release tension. Finding the rhythm we relax, our connection firm, our minds as one; in touch with our world, we dance!

Trouble and Beauty

Chris Loughlin

All peoples hold a belief, a story of how the world came to be. That belief or story gives meaning and purpose to our lives and we derive our ethics and first principles from that meaning. The marvel of our time is the awesome observations that have been bestowed upon us. We are the first generations to observe that we do not live in a spatial or one-time created universe. With "new eyes and new ears" extended through telescope and radio wave we see and hear our oneness with an evolving journey of 15 billions years. The universe story has been one of irreversible transformative moments guided and spawned by the primal acts of the universe itself, always moving toward greater complexity, deeper interiority and more intimate communion.

We arrive at this new millenium in the midst of planetary crisis. From a scientific point of view Earth is at a turning point in its evolutionary process. From a spiritual perspective life has reached a point of breakthrough in the creation process. The new scientific discoveries of the last half of the twentieth century have become the voices of modern prophets offering insights and critique, holding forth hope and promise to a culture that chooses death and diminishment over creation and life.

Our women's work is crucial in this spiritual breakthrough. For eons our strength and gifts have been the capacity to sense, feel, intuit, be present to the suffering of others, heal the brokenhearted and invite wholeness where there is division. Now we see with new eyes and hear with new ears that the suffering and separations and losses are planetary. It is the children of all species that are at great risk. Our own separation from the community of the natural world is intrinsic in the great suffering of Earth.

According to Robin Morgan, writer, poet, journalist, and feminist leader, the courage required decades ago for feminists to name the already existing divisions between men and women, the separation, the anguish, and the courage required to relate that division to all the other separations based on race, age, nationality, and others, would need to be squared in order to accomplish this naming of the already existing integration that connects, surrounds, and embraces us all. Once we struggled to name the separations; now we work even harder to recognize that everything that exists is intimately connected with every expression of the creation.

> By these hearts of rage we have come thus far,
> to this place in our love where we dare ....
> trouble and beauty, we dare trouble, we
> dare beauty and that far wondering star still
> calls us on.[1]

Our women's work awakened us. Now the journey must take us far beyond reflecting and acting on behalf of women's experiences. Our capacity to hold the collective suffering has drawn us toward a planetary consciousness, a place we never expected. We see that our holding actions of the past decades have led to creative work on behalf of the planet itself. We have drawn our energy to land based projects, come home to place, organized within our local ecosystem and begun to recreate human culture with an intimate awareness of the life support system of our home planet. This involvement with our lands is not just a romantic endeavor, not something personal for pleasure. Our movement now is the reshaping of human culture through the reinventing of agri-culture, the creation of legal rights for watersheds, the care and improvement of soils as source of all life, human, plant, and animal, the defense of the habitat of the children of all species in a "neighborhood."

We are at the threshold of Earth's revelatory moment. An evolution in creation is near. We prepare ourselves to participate in this transforming act.

The Spirit is even now disrupting the old patterns of thinking and engaging us in holy chaos. The land is the medium where Spirit will speak, the natural world expressed in the multiform community of beings that have come the long process of creation. This evolutionary breakthrough will not be biological but conscious, psychic. The revelatory moments will come to those most attentive, most aware, most compassionate with the whole community of Being in its suffering and anguish. Our rage will dare us into the truth of our own denial and devastation; our Woman's love will recognize the Beauty of a new order that embraces with enlightened compassion our oneness in this tough spun web.[2]

---

[1] From *Trouble and Beauty* by Carolyn McDade
[2] From *This Tough Spun* Web by Carolyn McDade

Within Her Loose and Sure Embrace

Carolyn McDade

Unexpected, from places unseen, they bolt upon the path with the directness of a hawk upon some movement in still grass. They come in a startling moment when something opens and we see in a new way what has been there all the time. One thing is clear. A revelatory moment is a mystery and a gift. In its long slow instant, everything is made different.

I passed the high rising boulder as I always did. This time, however, something made me stop and turn back to the smooth upreaches of its breadth. It was the last day of an annual retreat of solitude and silence on the rocky shore of the North Atlantic. As I prepared to return home to the activist life I both chose and felt claimed by, I left my packing to make my rounds of gratitude and farewell to the places where my mind had slowly quietened enough to lie fresh and open to a deeper listening.

Each day I had walked by this giant rock on my way to the low places at water's edge. I felt at home there at tide level, where the ocean in the rhythm of eons, poured its restless waters upon a shore of stone—waves shattering into fields of diamonds, spinning sun through a whirl of lenses and scattering light and wetness upon all within their reign of wonder.

Whatever in my leave-taking made me turn from the flying spray of the low ledges to climb above the tides, I do not know. Yet I turned without hesitation. Alone in the early morning I made my way up the sloping side of the giant rock, mammoth among its neighbors. As I climbed, the world around me quietened, stretching a quilt of calm upon the roar below. Even the wind, strong from its run over open waters, could not breach the assemblage of peace. I felt I had come in surprise upon some ancient temple where all things breathed and all breathing created one breath.

Beneath my feet, the boulder that had turned me from my path and brought me climbing up its flank, over its shoulder and onto its broad back, was suddenly more than stone. It was a heartbeat rising above the waves that pounded its sides and filled the caves beneath its belly—a being of the sea and of the shore. Held aloft by this giant one and following what I knew its eyes would have me see, I looked out into the expanse of grayblue sea, the immensity from which each wave, each wing of diamonds, lifts and to which it returns. Slowly my sight moved across to the *long arm of horizon* holding this ocean. The same arm that held the waters reached and took my eyes and with steady deliberateness swept them around the long curve of her nature.

From the far left of her northern stretch round to the south, and without pause circling on around the rocks to all behind them—the stubble of treetops, the drops and reaches of this craggy shore, a land of creatures and people with their purposes and their children and dreams, their imaginings beyond the farthest tomorrow. Steadily, silently, the line of wrinkles and points swung, sliding off the shore, back to the smoothness of distant sea, returning to the place from which I had begun this turn of horizon.

It was a simple movement of the body in a landscape generous with magnitude, plainness and mystery, its unspoken and infinitely revealed faithfulness, each taking its place in the saga of earth, in the drama of universe. Tears flooded my eyes, filled my being. From the center of that moment, within its wholeness, some larger self spoke—*I am your teacher now.*

The woman who stepped off that rock was different from the one who had turned back to walk upon it. The horizon came with me, her long line attaching a birthing cord to my body, connecting me with the lifeline of her existence, holding me within her loose and sure embrace, infusing me with her faith in the worthiness of this journey called creation.

Over and over I have found myself, in places different one from the other, turning the circle of horizon, opening my body, my being, to the fullness of turning in that moment, in that place. Each horizon has been a holding place embracing all within her curve. Each also has been a crossing from the known into the unknown, the seen into the unseen. Each has offered teachings of certitude and mystery, assurance and risk. Each has been an invitation to move toward that which one reaches by intention and enters by letting go. Horizon both separates and unites, for what is beyond is held in the arm of the beyond. What I know is that she calls us to wider meanings, to a deeper self, inseparable from the destiny of all within her hold and beyond her crossing. Within her arm our lives, like waves on stone, disintegrate into a wing of diamonds. We are without boundaries in the currents of life. We are never severed, though over and over we lose our way.

***

Most of my life has been lived in the twentieth century, a span of years frequented by humanity losing its way. I was born on the heels of the Great Depression, was a child in World War II. People my age have known a world of war, violence, cruelty, destruction, disparity, exploitation and the grave features of human injustice that both spawn and are spawned by such a reality. We have lived within social structures and ways of relating built on domination, hierarchy, and the assumptions, attitudes, and deliberate misuse of power that hold such a status quo in place as normative.

Yet within this tragic century there has been an amazing awakening. The flowering of liberation movements, the connecting of justice with peace, the development of nonviolence as a social movement and a way of life, a growing grassroots compassion for other people and beings, a deepening understanding of our participation in a vast web, and all that has come from seeing our earth from space for the first time.

Within this context the consciousness of women has opened globally with ferocity and beauty, horizon upon horizon breaking like waves one upon another. It has released profound psychic, physical, and creative energies—intelligence, intuition, emotion, and imagination, together with the courage each of these requires to be honest and transformative. Around the world women have begun to see their lives, societies, and world in ways they had not seen them before. We are women on the long trek back to ourselves, continuing what was begun before our time.

Within this story are many particularities. What I share are my thoughts from the strand of stream in which I found myself; I do not attempt to generalize an awakening as diverse and far reaching as the one I've just described.

In the early feminism of my life, women gathered at the boundary of institutions in which we lacked significant envisioning and decision-making power. Here we were able to maintain control of what we did and how we did it. In these circles we spoke and listened as we had never done before. We told our stories, found their patterns, analyzed, studied, wept, sang, we made plans of action and we acted. We scrutinized patriarchy, creating within its status quo a field of feminist query.

This boundary place became a place of truth telling, of sharing rage, fear, sorrow, and love—the unraveling of all that denied us life and the astonishing emergence of what it meant to be ourselves, women blessed by life's affirmation that we live with integrity and fullness. We worked ritual and vision like clay, shaping and reshaping them to honour the authenticity of women, and to affirm our experiences and truths. Thus we formed a spirituality of affirmation and blessing, and the beginning of a culture that inspired, sustained, and celebrated our lives.

From these circles we returned to life in the larger culture. All that had been created on the boundary came with us. Thus began the creative interweaving of boundary with the longstanding institutions. The boundary brought an emphasis on integrity, inclusion, mutuality, participation, revisioning, and change. The institutions rested in their social power and their claim to holding and interpreting definitive truth and what is normative and what is deviant within the culture. Some places were open to dialogue and change; others were not. But our lives as women were changed forever.

From our perspectives as women with our own moral agency we scrutinized everything that touched on our bodies and sexuality, our rights to integrity and choice. We were intent on full participation in naming reality, raising questions, establishing priorities, and envisioning the future. We critiqued war, economics, politics, theology and religion, and the *compulsory heterosexuality* (a term used by feminist poet/writer Adrienne Rich) of our culture. We were concerned with the politics of the nation/state, the spreading power and lack of accountability of international corporations, nuclear weapons and energy, the rising global economy with its increase in disparity, disruption of local cultures, and devastation of the planet. We took feminist perspectives into the social movements seeking justice and peace among people. We began to reach across difference, learning to hear perspectives different from our own. We struggled with the knowledge of our own part in the oppression of other women and their peoples and the question of how this would change the way we lived. Slowly we began to see the ways that race, gender, social status/class, sexual identity/choice, age, nationality and religion interact to compound the effects of oppression in particular ways. Who decides? Who benefits? Who loses? What are the configurations of power and powerlessness?

These questions took on deeper meanings as we began to see humanity as part of the larger community of life. The horrific short and long-term effects of nuclear wastes emerging out of the technologies of war and energy sent us crashing into the reality of the devastating effects humanity was having upon the planet and all living things. Human ignorance, many times deliberately maintained by decision makers and by people reluctant to face the truth, colluded with human arrogance, fear, and greed to set us on a course of ever increasing speed toward the closing down of systems that form life on earth as we know it. Whose voices were being heard? What mindset produces such destructive attitudes and actions? As humanity we desperately needed not only a new action, but also a new consciousness out of which to see ourselves in relation to the whole of life.

Yet, through all our failings and regardless of the quality of our actions, the cord that binds creation together continues to do so, reminding us that all destinies are interwoven and no species or member of a species can opt out. The nature of this cord is one of generativity. It affirms, in grace, our human resource—our capacity to awaken to deeper understanding, to discern faithfulness from this place, and to live it with intention—bringing it into our everyday, close as a friend and a cup of tea, no more or less demanding than loving a child for whom we would turn the world upside down if need be.

Over and over in my adult life I have been blessed to circle with women reclaiming our lives and creativity. Within these circles I have experienced a consistency that I would describe as a collective desire to align our lives within the curve of a larger love—to create an arm of affirmation within our personal lives and our social institutions, to open ourselves to what it means to be in right relationship as personal, social, and planetary beings, bringing our fullness of being to serve the well-being of the whole. It means creating and recreating the culture we need to become this humanity.

***

In late August 1999 more than eighty women crossed mountains, prairies, woodlands, to gather at The Banff Centre for the Arts in the Canadian Rocky Mountains of Alberta. We were there as a part of the project *We Are the Land We Sing*, to record the music, put together a quilt, write our experiences, and to find our way collectively into

Sacred Web, the name we had come to call ourselves. We came representing local groups of women who for a year had met to sing, reflect, and give creative expression to the interrelating of land and spirit in our lives as women.

We gathered for the first time on Sunday evening, most of us after long hours, even days, of travel. By Monday afternoon we were on risers in the large new recital hall having our first sound check in the place where the following day we would begin recording. Although the centre staff welcomed us warmly and our engineers were encouraging and skilled, we felt lost to ourselves as a community. The hall was cavernous and intimidating, headphones a challenge, the experience of recording new to us, and most of us did not know the singers from regions other than our own. We had the music in common but we had set up our own local ways of working with it.

Monday evening all plans to rehearse were laid aside. Two among us who were experienced in community building, opened the circle and invited us to talk together about what we were experiencing and what we needed in order to continue. Even in the stress of knowing how much we had to do in the next five days, spaciousness spread among the group as we shared feelings and ideas. To make the recording space our own we decided to move our altar there. We would take time to become acquainted with the hall by walking and quietly forming a relationship with its space. Well into our discussion that evening a woman of the prairie spoke. *As it is, we each do not sing on all songs. When we are not the ones recording we are free to do other things. But this music belongs to all of us. Those of us who are not recording should remain in the hall and form a circle of witness around those who are.*

This act became the defining character of our week. As we formed this circle around others singing, we knew in some deep place that we were there to do more than watch. We gathered in the profound human act of bearing witness, being fully present, with that presence being a vital participation in the creation of the whole. It was a human act resonant with the way of wider energies—a forming of the arm of affirmation, a curve of intentional assurance around that within its hold.

Over days, as women moved between recording and witnessing, we came to understand the vital difference between coming to stand in a circle and coming to take one's place there. Within the whole we began to see in a new way. Instead of looking at trees standing outside the large recital hall windows, we began to feel their presence, the long ancestry that brought them there, and the arm of mountains beyond them. To be in their presence, lifted by the heartbeat of the land, connected our voices to the profound motivations that brought us there—to create culture that deepens human understanding and strengthens our commitment to create sustainable ways of living that reverence the earth, one another, and the wider community of beings with which we share life and habitat.

What happened was not a step into some golden arena of ideal perfection. We were living under demands that made most of our acts simply the ones that were spontaneous. We still had misunderstandings and differing perspectives. There was not the time or means to talk things through or step back and consider, other than that remarkable Monday night gathering and the informal times many had together. Yet something within our community allowed all of this to be within the circle without tilting the whole away from our collective intent. The deep centerings by which various clusters of women brought us together each morning were a strong part of creating trust and a common ground. To this day I remember with amazement the openness and visibility of our lives. Within this transparency moved our imperfections and our shining capacity to hold loosely a circle of stunning generosity. The cord of Creation, pulsing with life, joined us body to body with the mountains and the trees and all that we loved. It connected the gentle and gifted women leading us in song with each singer, each singer with the path of heart between and among us, together generating the stamina to continue on.

These are stories we must never forget—the times and ways we create a passage for humanity that calls forth our deepest and best, enabling us to remain intact through all that would provoke a cleavage in our communal will.

***

It has been a decade of earth crisis since I walked onto that boulder looking out upon the sea. Now, in the scant and perfect light of this midwinter afternoon, I come to the bay to place myself again in the elemental energies of the planet, this time in the land I call home. It has become a ritual in my life to come and lean into a larger wisdom to guide me in what I do.

The beach glistens, smooth and firm from winter tides, soon to be covered again. Across the inlet of Wellfleet Harbor and beyond the distant rising of Great Hill Island, the bay gathers and dispenses the cold waters of the North Atlantic, its channels at times frequented by whale and sea turtle, dolphin, and the horseshoe crab who come to mate each May and to lay eggs in the sands at water's edge. This land is alive in the creative process by which all elements and beings interact with one another to form habitats. Humanity, each of us in our personal and collective ways, is a part of this, whether consciously or unconsciously, whether with reverence or reckless disregard.

Among these relations I stand upon this planet, within her warm and intimate curve, her arm full of water. My feet on sand wet from tides and early rain, I slowly turn the circle of this horizon, rounding island and harbor, beach and cliff, the curve of bay, full circle. I bow.

I bow to the heartbeat of life within this place and all beings of this place, within all who take this world in our arms like a lover, her water our blood, her rock our bone, her long voice our song, her saga the story out of which we rise, her formation the instruction for our struggles, her earth time that which will humble our own swift carelessness.

I pray to this land, the rise and fall of waters, the high arched heaven. I pray to the shallows and the depths, all the life that manages its flutter of time in one or the other or both. I pray to the sun that lifted the morning's rain, and now dries the stones and pours its ecstasy upon the seal. I pray to the stand of pitch pine that lines this shore, trees gnarled and wizened, crusty and limber to the wind. I pray to those who have gone before. I reverence their grace and imperfection, each shining tally of goodness in a broken world. I pray to those who remain, to those who will come after, those of the morrows beyond tomorrow.

I pray we learn to curve our hearts in the curve of her arm, which rests in the curve of planets within the curve of the Milky Way and clustered galaxies, reaching back through the generations of supernovas and primal stars, to the curve of beginnings, to the *throb in the first orb* that birthed this universe, flinging the invisible cord into all directions, times, and entities, seeding with possibility a universe of opening embrace.

I pray we hold tenderly and fiercely this unbroken story of the vast and the minute, remembering to tell its wonders, how the great orb moves in the curve of heart and grass and a drop of water, in the curve of each cell and spiraling DNA throbbing with life, reproducing, continuing, changing, continuing, greening, flowering, continuing a planet and all beings formed by and forming the community of creation. This story belongs to all beings. We do not own it. It forms in the arena of cosmic participation. It comes from the integrity of the whole, and thus is beyond possession.

Our lives and creativity are a part of this dynamic formation, this miracle of sacred emerging. The creating of human culture hums with the energy that creates habitats on earth and galaxies in space. This relatedness and our reverence for it call us as humanity to weave together our creativity and life purpose for the well-being of the whole.

I call forth these wisdoms in life -
the circle of horizon and the circle of witness
the arm of social movement and the open embrace affirming the whole
the cord of the first orb's quiver,
unbroken love birthing tomorrow from this day.
I bow.
May I be faithful. May we together be.

There Is a Time

© 1995 by Carolyn McDade

There is a time that we must rise There is a
There is a time that we must leave Go from the

time that we must stand There is a time that we must
place where ha-treds breed and, turn - ing, feel the Spir-it

come to - ge - ther For bless – ed
breathe us to - ge - ther

are our lives Bless - ed our love and

bless - ed the pro - mise gath - ered now

There Is A Time

Carolyn McDade

There is a time that we must rise
There is a time that we must stand
There is a time that we must come together

for blessed are our lives
blessed our love
blessed the promise gathered now

There is a time that we must leave
Go from the place where hatreds breed
and, turning, feel the Spirit breathe us together

There is a time we know the way
There is a time, we watch and pray
In living faith we make our way
together

Upon the dry a cloud will rise
and truth will shine among the lies
and wisdom sing
as we arise together

There is a bow within the rain
and it will come and bend again
and colours shine
where we have been together

Blessed are our lives
Blessed our love
Blessed the promise gathered now

Afterword

Dianne Linden

April 20, 2001
Jasper, Alberta

I sit on a rock above the Athabasca River. It's the time of year when the ancient conversation between water and ice begins again in earnest. The river opens a channel for free-running discussion. Ice flows down-river, fills the channel in and the sound of running water stops. Activity continues somewhere under the surface of the ice, however, because in time, a new channel responds to water's insistence, and the spring voice of the river rises again to where I sit basking like a winter-weary ground hog, sun-dazzled and newly reacquainted with the world of light.

I don't know what to call the colour the river's wearing today: whether it's turquoise or azure or some ancient and unnamable shade of green. But I've carried this same colour away in memory from the mountains of British Columbia, Colorado, Montana, and Norway. It's a resource I call on for dealing with depression and general world-weariness. And I'm reassured that despite the growing belief in water as a commodity to be bottled and sold to anyone thirsty [and rich] enough, water herself is still apolitical in adornment and presentation.

Beside me is the almost-final draft of a collection of writing that has been two years in gestation. I look once more at the luminescent Athabasca as she opens and closes in negotiation before me, then turn to this other river of women's words and experience. *Running Barefoot*, the title sings to me. I know enough about making my way through life bare-so[u]led to understand the implications of this naming. Bare feet are feet that can ignore neither the luxuriant smoothness of mud, nor the painful impediment of thorns and rocks. Bare feet are feet that feel every centimetre of a journey. And so it is for the writers whose journeys we glimpse within the pages of this book. This is truly barefoot writing.

Despite the rigorous and enforced training in domesticity women have endured for millennia, these writers are very close to the wildness I am surrounded by today. Somehow they have relearned and reowned what it is like to smell the sky, to hear the rush of saltwater in their blood, to carry the languorous haze of Autumn in their souls and dance with Winter in a theatre as large as the North herself. Standing in the presence of that which is entirely foreign to them, entirely other, they do not attempt to name or collect and order it. Unlike the explorers who mapped their sorry egos and financial interests all over the pristine western face of this country, these writers do not desire domination. Rather, in the face of great awe, they seek to establish relationship. Sometimes that relationship speaks of the connectedness and nurturance of mother and child, sometimes of enthrallment, or healing or preparation for death.

They also demonstrate what must be an intentional art in a frenetic post-modern world that bombards us with reminders of the passing of time: credit, dinner, even our skin's absorption of hand lotion must be instant because we don't have time to wait. These writers, however, whether through counter-cultural intention or giftedness, wait with grace and even relish—for the birth of a child or a calf, for the opening of a flower, for bones to become earth, for the silence of rock and water to enter them and speak.

Perhaps because of their ability to live outside linear or chronus time, they read in the earth neither strata nor striation nor the names of scientific eras, but an interweaving of memories and stories. These are valuable skills to be passed on to our children—more valuable than a great deal of the enforced learning mandated by public school curricula. Perhaps some of these writers will also embrace the task of teacher. The land has already provided the school.

Is it coincidence, I wonder, that this connection to wildness should be found in so many women writers? (And I add in the next breath that) my question arises not from a desire to be exclusive, but from the need to better understand this group I number myself within. Do we, perhaps, have a unique relationship with the land itself: wild and in cultivation?

Some of the women in this collection write as though they are earth—their veins the gold that miners seek and artisans fashion into jewelry; their bodies as birth-givers and passageways. Certainly as women we know what it is to be plowed and seeded and harvested. Throughout his/story our bodies have been entered and exited; often broken into. For centuries the lived-experience of millions of women has consisted of being opened up, examined, cross-examined, tortured and interrogated. As women we have been revered for our innocence and saintliness; made the objects of fetishist devotion for our beauty, desirability and fecundity; censored and despised for our sensuality, waywardness, barrenness, cronism and witchery.

And still:

there is a fundamental wildness within us that cannot be controlled unless we, ourselves, allow it: that cannot be camped or hiked upon, cross-country skied over, spelunked or helicoptered into; there is a persistent wildness that sees land not in terms of what it can bare, but in the beauty of its sparseness, and even in the severity of its failure to provide; there abides this primal wildness that weeps and howls and gnashes its teeth at the prospect of the land's desecration.

I believe in this wildness: I find it a cause for great hope.

I celebrate its presence in the words and music that fill this volume. If we turn to it with intention, first to heal each other, and then to run and walk and write and dance and sing that healing bare-so[u]led out onto the land, what a transformation that would create. If we allow it to, this wildness can help us resist cultural pressures to commodify and commercialize even the most sacred places. *If we allow it*, it will attune us to injustices against the land and all those who call it home.

I wonder. If the women writing in this anthology had the legislative power to protect the remaining wildness in this country, would so many of our national parks be in crisis today? Would Banff be criss-crossed with four lane highways where foxes and porcupines and even grizzlies are continually slaughtered? Would the headwaters of the Bow River that rise there, be laced with chemical toxins? Would up-market shopping malls compete with the grandeur of the mountains for the attention of millions of tourists who pass through each year in the wake of even more millions of pop cans, plastic six-pack containers and cellophane wrappers?

The American poet, Mary Oliver wrote, *I don't know exactly what a prayer is. I do know how to pay attention, how to fall down into the grass, how to kneel down into the grass, how to be idle and blessed . . .*[1] To say I am reassured by the prayerful attention of many of the writers in this collection is too faint a statement. Rather, I am enheartened that as I write this in the Spring presence of a mountain

---

[1] Mary Oliver. "The Summer Day," New and Selected Poems. Boston: Beacon Press, 1992, p. 94.

river, another woman stands prayerfully as her eye adjusts to the visual impact of a single purple crocus in a winter-bleached field. I am energized that other women sit in contemplation beside the ocean, their breathing an act of worship. I am humbled that women walk and sing the Grandmother Hills in the Qu'Appelle Valley to assist us in the final work of editing this anthology. Until recently I did not know these women were there.

Now I understand that all across this land women bear daily witness to the presence of the holy in whose daily re—creation we are generously involved. Now I understand that women all across this land mourn the small deaths that go unnoticed in a culture bent on creating an excess of sensation and material possessions. These women grieve the death of each animal killed and left beside the highway: of small spaces held sacred in the memories of children: of the habitat lost to each species of plant or animal that finds itself displaced by our culture's insatiable need for more at any cost.

And the cost is high. If it involves the bones of even one more mountain, or the blood of one more river, it is already higher than we can imagine.

These thoughts visit me as I keep my vigil beside the Athabasca River. Meanwhile she continues to create new channels in the ice. The ice resists and fills them in again. The river yields to this momentary obstruction, but in time offers yet another opportunity for movement. The Spring break-up of river ice is an event Northerners know as well as breathing. We need to know more about what we can learn from witnessing such an ancient ritual. How can we, like the river itself, move our beliefs out into the world, despite obstacles and opposition? This is the most difficult of questions. It's one the writers in this collection struggle with more than any other.

How can we live into what we write or sing or dream?

There are no easy answers; none that are guaranteed not to inconvenience us or bring change into our comfortable and predictable lives. After all, it is so much easier to be moved than to be movers.

And yet that's what the crisis of the land calls us to do.

We must find a way to take all we have sensed and felt and wept and laughed over and written and sung, and move it forward. We must carry the liquid of our private conversations into places that do not welcome movement. And when that process meets impediment, we must be insistent in the way of spring rivers—offering, yielding; offering, yielding. It's a small task with a narrow focus: one that can be managed by every single woman who takes heart from these words and this music.

Carolyn McDade often shares this saying with women: "We must go slowly. There is not much time."[2] There is as much apparent opposition in those words as there is in the nature of water and ice. Yet each pair of opposites is born of the same essence. As writers and readers of this text, and as bare-so[u]led travelers of this land, we can come to understand the mysteries of that opposition. And naming the resistances we face while maintaining day by day persistence, we can make a difference.

It's a small undertaking when measured a task at a time. It's only a small undertaking and yet

everything depends upon it.

---

[2] Ms. McDade attributes this saying to the Women's Theological Center in Boston.

Contributors

Ingrid Alesich is a woman of many races, a teacher, and one who strives to be open to learning about life, love and fear, in all their complexities. She lives in Saskatchewan, on a northern plateau of prairie expanses, boreal forest and lakes, a land of ice and gentle warmth. The earth is her inspiration and her touchstone.

Kelsey Andrews is a young woman who lives and writes in the country near Grande Prairie, Alberta. Her writing has been previously published in *Persephone's Sisters: Young Women Write (Rowan Books, 2000)*, in a Peace Region anthology edited by Elroy Deimert, Smoky Peace Press.

Luanne Armstrong is a Kootenay writer now located in Vancouver, who is completing an MFA in creative writing at the University of British Columbia. She is a widely published author and is also managing editor of Hodgepog Books. In the fall of 2000 she was writer in residence at Berton House in Dawson City, Yukon.

Willow Barton says: I was born in Red Pheasant, Saskatchewan. It was called *Yellow Sky* when my people came there a very long time ago. My father was from the Black Hills. I am sometimes a writer of Cree stories and sometimes an artist, but always I am interested in presenting stories that explore my people's circumstances.

Jacqueline Bell lives and writes in Edmonton. *Burning for it*, her first book of poetry, was published by Rowan Books in 1998.

Doris Bircham has been partnered with the same man, same ranch in the Cypress Hills of southwestern Saskatchewan, and the same prairie wind, forever. She has been a feature performer at many cowboy poetry gatherings, and in the video, *Cowboy Poetry: Words to Live By* produced by Mediatalk Productions in 1996. Her work has been published in magazines, anthologies and aired on radio and TV.

Ruth Blaser is a woman of the prairie. She lives with her partner Brenda MacLauchlan, a woman of the ocean, and Rebekah, a girl of the stars. Ruth loves to give her energy to creating sustainable lives, land and cultures. She enjoys singing and reflecting in circles of women.

Carol Yamabe Breitkreutz lives in Camrose, Alberta, with her husband, two teenage children, two cats and a dog. She is a teacher by profession and an artist by heart. She enjoys creating in many forms including the Spirit Women Dolls she wrote about for this collection.

Audrey Brooks was born on the Saskatchewan prairie but now lives in Edmonton where she shares gifts from Gaia by singing, facilitating writing circles, and practicing pastoral ministry. She stays connected with the land through Taoist Tai Chi, wilderness camping, and photography. She is a graduate of the University of Alberta and of Bangor Theological Seminary in Bangor, Maine.

Rebecca Campbell lives and writes on Vancouver Island. She has published her writing in numerous Canadian literary magazines and is working on her first poetry collection.

Ruth Cey lives on a farm near Wilkie, Saskatchewan, with her husband and four children. She teaches high school part time, has written educational materials for elementary school children, and children's books, including *What Would You Call This Sky?* In 1996 she won "How To Survive a Saskatchewan Winter" poetry contest (CBC Radio, Saskatchewan).

p k chamberlain is an English instructor at Augustana's Centre for Community Education in Camrose, Alberta. She grew up in the farming community of Tulliby Lake, north of Lloydminster.

Sylvia Chetner has lived most of her life on the western Canadian prairies. She began writing after a career as a librarian.

Martha Cole is a professional fabric artist, calligrapher, teacher and bookbinder/artist living in Saskatchewan. She believes that when created with honouring and respectful intention, both text and image carry within them the power to bring about change. Her machine-stitched and quilted works, which have been exhibited nationally and internationally, are celebratory of our planet.

Madeleine Dahlem is a full time high school teacher in Saskatoon. She began to write ten years ago, finally making a commitment to a childhood dream.

Judy Delorme offers this by way of saying who she is: I am Granddaughter, Cree Granddaughter. I am daughter, Cree daughter. I am woman, Cree woman. I am Grandmother, Cree Grandmother.

Diane Driedger divides her time between Winnipeg and Trinidad. Her poetry has appeared in *Queen's Quarterly, Prairie Fire, Whetstone* and *Contemporary Verse 2*. A book of her poetry, *The Mennonite Madonna*, was published by gynergy books in 1999.

Heather Duff has been widely published in Canadian literary magazines, among them *Grain, The Antigonish Review, Descant* and *Phoenix Rising*. She is currently editor/director for Vancouver Youth Theatre's Kids' Writes project, in which the creative writing of young authors is selected to be dramatized for a school tour throughout the Lower BC Mainland.

Candace Duiker is a young woman who lives and writes in Edmonton. This is her first published poem. She has been writing for one year and loves the places where poetry takes her.

Wynne Edwards Her previous editing experience includes *Study in Grey: Women Writing about Depression*, and *Taking off the Tinsel*, both published by Rowan Books. She stays connected to the land by walking in an area of undeveloped river valley and by writing in a retreat-like setting east of Edmonton.

Elsie Ellis has retired to the family farm located in Hazlet, Saskatchewan, on the eastern edge of the Great Sand Hills. Her poetry is solidly rooted in the prairie around her. A member of the Range Writers, she has often appeared with the cowboy poets at Regina's Agribition, and is a regular at the Maple Creek Gathering. Her third book of poetry, *The Land of My Undoing*, was published in 1998.

Jean Fahlman and her husband live on a farm in Griffith, Saskatchewan, where they have recently harvested their fiftieth crop together. She has written a weekly newspaper column since 1971, has served in the Saskatchewan Writers Guild and is president of the Weyburn Writers Group. Her work has appeared in a wide range of papers, magazines and anthologies, and has received numerous awards.

Mary Gazetas lives in Richmond, BC. She has paddled the coast with her twin sister, Phoebe and family for over eighteen summers. An artist, writer and grandmother, she has published several articles in national and regional heritage, travel and paddling periodicals. Mary is currently working on a book, *Around One More Point*, which captures the beauty of the British Columbia coast and her paddling journeys.

Vivian Hansen touches rocks and navigates grass maps to find ripe Saskatoon bushes. She is also a hunter, which demands total spiritual engagement with nature, wind, and the animal that gives up its spirit. Vivian's nonfiction has appeared in *Threshold, Our Grandmothers, Ourselves*, and *Study in Grey*.

Cathy Hodgson grew up in the Northwest Territories in a mining camp. She lives and writes in Edmonton.

Linda Wikene Johnson has an MFA in Creative Writing from the University of British Columbia. She has published one collection of poetry, *Showcase Animals*, which deals with her experiences living in northern B.C. She has had short stories, novellas and poems published by *Windsor Review, Dalhousie Review, Event, The Canadian Fiction Magazine, Prism International* and many others.

Lois Kennedy has lived, worked and played in nature since childhood. Her deep connection with Nature has been expressed in a lifetime of outdoor sports and recreation, as a research scientist, a tapestry artist, and in teaching and lay ministry. Her life is now dedicated to stream and watershed stewardship on Gambier Island, where she lives, and to singing in community with a group of women who call themselves the Sacred Web.

Dianne Linden is a teacher, editor, writer, and grandmother. She has lived in Edmonton for the past thirty-two years, yet she still thinks of the mountains as home. Only recently has she learned to see in the meeting place of flat land and wide blue sky another kind of blessing.

Chris Loughlin is a Dominican Sister who lives and works at Crystal Spring Center for Earth Learning. Crystal Spring gives voice to the need for open space and the resacrilization of land, agriculture and community. Her primary work is guiding a learning center where workshops and retreats provide time for people to study the New Cosmology and to awaken to the values and skills needed to reconnect with the natural world.

Nancy Mackenzie keeps her ear to the ground. Her four published books include a book of poetry, called *Soul's Flight* (Ekstatis Editions, 1997).

Catherine MacLean has a degree from Harvard, a certificate in Dogrib (one of the Dene languages of the subarctic), and nine years of experience as a parent, for which, apparently, no diploma is issued.

Heather MacLeod is a member of the Metis Nation Northwest Territories. She grew up in British Columbia, Alberta, the Yukon and the Northwest Territories. Although she no longer lives in Yellowknife, she still considers it home. Her work has appeared in *Grain, Fiddlehead, Prism International, Prairie Fire, Event* and *The Clay Palm Review*. Her first book of poetry, *My Flesh the Sound of Rain*, was published by Coteau Books in 1998.

Elaine Mann is a native Edmontonian who works as a music educator. Her love of nature and passion for song leading both began at the CGIT camps on Pigeon Lake and continue through leadership at various women's retreats. She was part of the song-leaders group for the taping of *We Are The Land We Sing* with Carolyn McDade and conducted We Shall Release a New Justice.

Mary Maxwell lives in Saskatoon. Her non-fiction has appeared in numerous Canadian literary magazines as well as in the anthologies: *Eating Apples, Knowing Women's Lives* (NeWest Press), and *Work and Leisure* (McGraw Hill). Her chapbook *Arrangements* was published by Hag Papers, Underwhich Editions in 1995. She is currently working on a collection of writing about grief.

Susan McCaslin teaches English and Creative Writing at Douglas College in Port Moody, British Columbia. She has published five volumes of poetry and expects to add two more to that list: one from University of Florida Press, and the other from Borealis Press in Ottawa.

Carolyn McDade is a lover of language and sound, and a writer of song. She is committed to the power of the human voice singing and speaking truth to move society to just and liberating transformation. She is also committed to deepening reverence for the web of life, and to strengthening our awareness that we are intimately interwoven with all that creates this living planet.

Melody McKellar was born and raised in Manitoba. She is a United Church minister who tries to follow her traditional aboriginal spirituality. Currently she lives and works in the Dr. Jesse Saulteaux Resource Center in Beausejour, MB.

Lorie Miseck lives in Edmonton, but was born and raised in Northern Alberta and on many days still yearns to sit quietly on the banks of the Peace River. Her work has appeared in a variety of journals and anthologies, and has been broadcast on CBC and WTN. She has one book of poetry, *the blue not seen*, published by Rowan Books.

Gwen Molnar is a much celebrated Edmonton poet, painter and writer of children's fiction. Most recently, she was shortlisted for the Alberta Writers Guild Award for children's Literature in 1997 for *Animal Rap and Far Out Fables*, and received the Canadian Authors Association's Exporting Alberta Award 2000 for *Sebastian's Promise*.

Claudia C. Morrison lives in Quebec in the winter and Ontario in the summer. She is the author of a novel, *From The Foot of The Mountain* (Cormorant) and a collection of stories, *I Should Know* (Morgaine House). Her poems have appeared in various Canadian journals; her first chapbook, *Arrival*, received the League of Canadian Poets Chapbook Award in 2000.

Kerry Mulholland lives and writes in Edmonton. The poems in this anthology are the first she has published.

Denise Needham is a 51 year old lesbian carpenter/business woman living on 160 acres just south of Regina Beach with her partner Lee. They run a bed and breakfast and retreat center. Denise writes to reduce feelings of isolation and to communicate feelings to people she is close to.

Therese Noonan farms with her husband in the Touchwood Hills of Saskatchewan where she writes about the animals and people in her life and their impact on her soul-that place where life and death meet. She believes our purpose in life is the unification of a living god with a dead one and the acknowledgement of our Mother as well as our Father.

Lia Pas is a composer, musician, singer, writer and yoga teacher living in Saskatoon. She performs with the Saskatoon Symphony and with the free-improv group DUCT. Her most recent publications are in *Zygote* and *Spring*, and in a chapbook, *vicissitudes*, published by Underwich Editions.

Monica Rosborough lives in Edmonton with her partner and two children, and enjoys kayaking, gardening and sacred clowning. This is her first published writing.

Eunice Victoria Scarfe, winner of the 2000 University of Alaska Short Fiction prize, is owner of Saga Seminars through which she offers writing workshops for women across North America.

Brenda Schmidt lives, writes and paints in northern Saskatchewan, in the mining community of Creighton, near Flin Flon, Manitoba. Two years ago she shed her previous life as a nurse to reveal a new skin that is scarred, but intact and healed. Her poetry has recently been published in *Zygote* and *Spring*.

Shirley A. Serviss is an Edmonton poet, essayist, freelance writer and adult educator. Her first published poetry collection, *Model Families*, was short-listed for Alberta Book of the Year. *Study in Grey: Women Writing About Depression* (Rowan Books, 1999) was co-edited by Serviss. *Reading between the Lines*, her second book of poetry, was published by Rowan Books in 2000.

Marian Shatto is an advocate for social justice, as well as a singer and musician involved in music ministry within the Moravian Church. She is a life-long resident of Pennsylvania. Her involvement with Carolyn's projects began in 1990 and continues to be a deeply enriching part of her life.

Theresa Shea has published poems in a number of journals, including *Queen's Quarterly, Matrix, Antigonish Review, CV2, Other Voices, Dandelion* and *NeWest Review*. She writes from her home in Edmonton where she is learning to identify the many plants and animals whose environment she shares.

Gayle Smith ranches with her husband and three children in Saskatchewan, where they have a growing herd of commercial and purebred cattle. She also raises and trains horses and gives lessons and clinics as a certified western riding coach. She juggles all this with her duties as a United Church minister who currently works as therapist/counsellor. She has published a book of cowgirl style poetry.

Lois Smith was born in rural Manitoba in 1940. She presently lives and works a few miles east of Winnipeg, Manitoba. Her love of the natural world led to the creation of her unique horseback riding program which offers women spiritual comfort through working with nature and horses.

Celeste N. Snowber Ph.D., is a writer, dancer and educator who has focused on the relationship between Eros, the body and the holy in the ordinary for twenty years. In addition to mothering three lively young boys, she is assistant professor in the Faculty of Education at Simon Fraser University. Celeste is author of *Embodied Prayer* and *In the Womb of God*, both published by Liguori in 1995.

Valerie Stetson is a poet whose work has appeared in many Canadian literary journals. She has worked as a humour columnist and TV writer for the *Times Colonist* in Victoria and has published articles in *The Globe and Mail* and *The Toronto Star*. Most recently she was awarded the 2001 Bronwen Wallace Award for short fiction. She now lives in Kelowna, BC.

Ardith Trudzik is a schoolteacher who has taken writing seriously since retiring and moving to Edmonton. She has a book in progress.

Lillian Vilborg has recently relocated to Manitoba, her birth place, following a long, happy period of her life in Edmonton, Alberta, where she was associated with the University of Alberta for over twenty-five years.

Debbie Voss was nurtured in her early years in the prairie community of Portage la Prairie, Manitoba before moving to Winnipeg. She is commissioned to diaconal ministry in the United Church of Canada and currently lives in Edmonton.

Bernadette L. Wagner lives with her family in Regina. She is a poet, mother, spouse, feminist, singer, activist, educator, and computer enthusiast, currently working on her first poetry manuscript. She hopes to have it published in her lifetime.

Joanna Weston was born in England and lives in Prince Albert with her husband, and near a daughter-in-law, three grandchildren, two cats and a growing garden. Her work has been widely published in Canada, the US and UK. Some of her poetry chapbooks include: *One of These Little Ones*, 1987, *Cuernavaca Diary*, 1990, *Seasons*, 1993 and *All Seasons*, 1996 (second edition 1997).

Christine Wiesenthal lives and works in Edmonton. Her poetry and creative non-fiction have appeared in such journals as *Grain, The New Quarterly, Room of One's Own, Dandelion* and on the CBC's *Alberta Anthology*. She has new poems forthcoming in *Descant* and *Queen's Quarterly*. Her first book of poetry, *Instruments of Surrender*, will appear with Buschekbooks in fall 2001.

Marianne Worcester was transplanted from the prairies to Vancouver in 1972. She is an instructor in a community college there and a summer dweller on Gambier Island. Her poetry and essays have appeared in *Sophia*, a Mennonite women's journal that voices women's experience in church, society, family and the workplace. She sings in community with a group of women who call themselves the Sacred Web.

Barb Yussack is a member of the Sacred Web singing group in Manitoba. For her, music has always been an important element in her spiritual healing journey. Barb dances and creates dance, sings and composes songs, chants and leads a drum circle for the women in her community. She creates ceremony to celebrate the rites of passage in life and shares her home with her two cats, Max and Micah.

Running Barefoot